The Ohio Gang

Also by Charles L. Mee, Jr.

BOOKS

White Robe, Black Robe

Erasmus

Daily Life in the Renaissance

Meeting at Potsdam

A Visit to Haldeman and Other States of Mind

Seizure

The End of Order: Versailles 1919

PLAYS

Players' Repertoire

Anyone! Anyone!

Constantinople Smith

Wedding Night

The Ohio Gang

THE WORLD OF WARREN G. HARDING

CHARLES L. MEE, JR.

M. EVANS
Lanham • New York • Boulder • Toronto • Plymouth, UK

M Evans
An imprint of Rowman & Littlefield
4501 Forbes Boulevard, Suite 200
Lanham, Maryland 20706
www.rowman.com

Library of Congress Cataloging in Publication Data

Mee, Charles L.
The Ohio gang.

Bibliography: p.243
Includes index.
1. Harding, Warren G. (Warren Gamaliel), 1865-1923.
2. Corruption (in politics)–United States. 3. United States–Politics and government–1921-1923. 4. Presidents–United States–Biography. I. Title. II. Title: The world of Warren G. Harding.

E786.M23 973.91′4′0924 [B] 81-3252

ISBN 978-1-59077-287-4 AACR2

Distributed by
NATIONAL BOOK NETWORK

DESIGN BY RONALD F. SHEY

Manufactured in the United States of America

For Herb Katz

Picture research by MEREDITH M. COLLINS.

All photographs from BROWN BROTHERS
except where otherwise credited.

Contents

The Twenties

The Twenties, A Portfolio

1. Miss America, 1921
2. The boys come marching home, through Madison Square, New York
3. The Babe
4. In grandpa's lap, listening to the new radio
5. Miss Mary Pickford
6. Charlie Chaplin and Jackie Coogan in *The Kid*
7. Corn-on-the-cob and a hot dog at Coney Island
8. Howard Wilcox, winner of the Indy 500, in his Peugeot Special
9. Atlantic City bathing beauties
10. Women vote, for the first time

11, 12, and 13. Prohibition agents Izzy and Moe, the still, and the speakeasy

14 and 15. The Klan

16. Wall Street, bombed by non-traders
17. Sacco and Vanzetti
18. Philadelphia strikers, broken

19 and 20. Hoboes

21. The family on Sunday in their Model T
22. Mt. Vernon Avenue, near the home of Mr. and Mrs. Warren G. Harding, in Marion, Ohio

1.

2.

3.

4.

5.

6.

7.

8.

9.

27

10.

TO

12.

11.

13.

14.

15.

BUCKS
COUNTY
PENNSYLVANIA

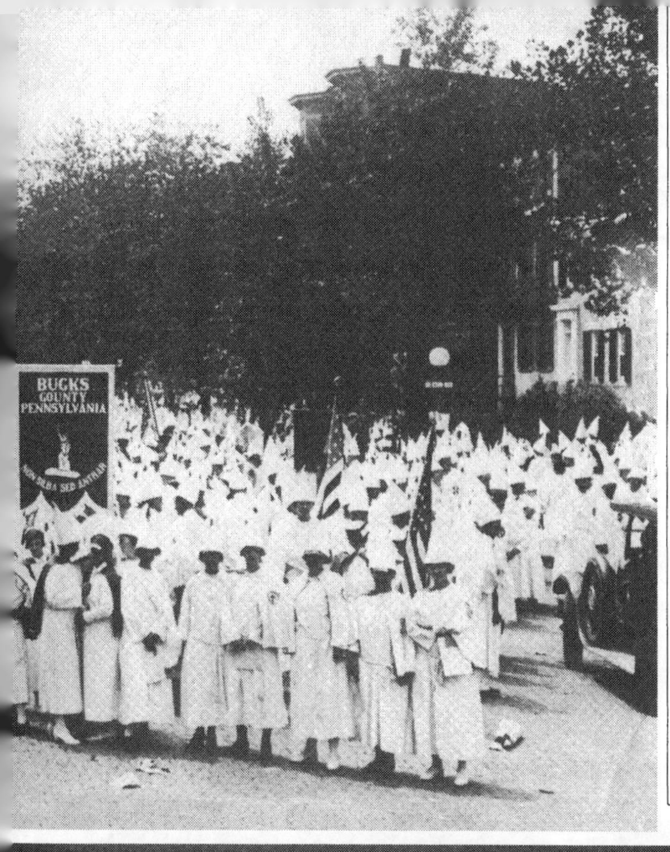

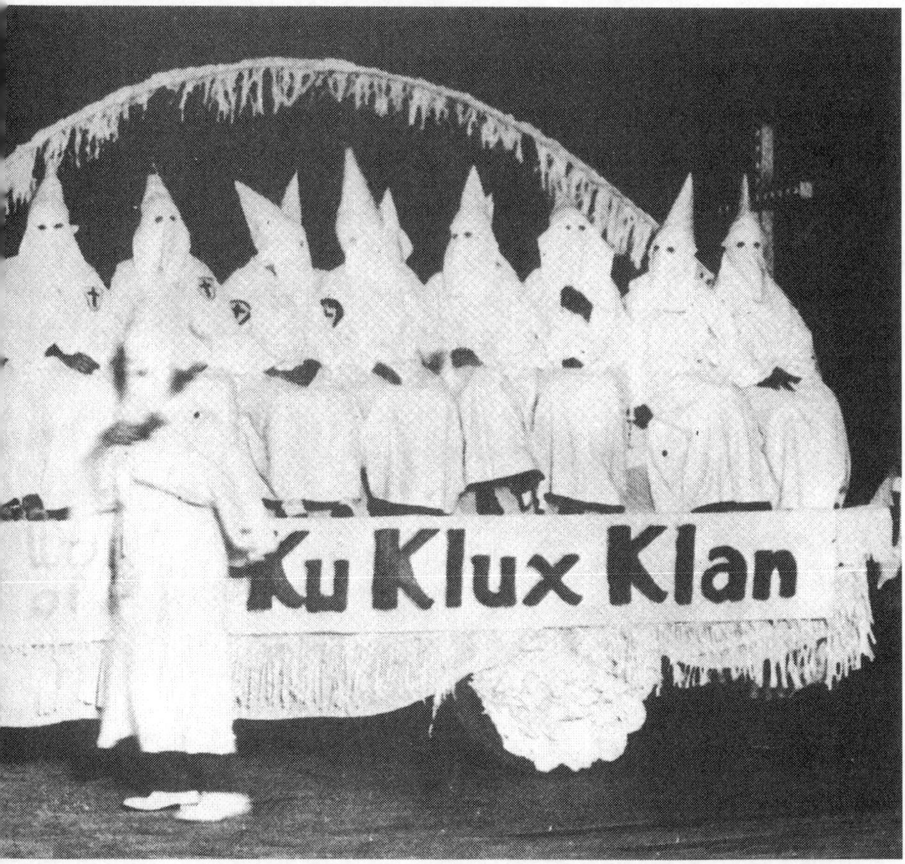
Ku Klux Klan

16.

17.

18.

19.

20.

21.

22.

The Ohio Gang

The Handshake

IN MIDWEEK, THE last week of May 1921, Jess Smith stood talking to another man just off Times Square, in the Astor Hotel lobby next to the entrance to the American Indian dining room with its crossed spears, peace pipe, snowshoes, horned headdress of a Tlingit chief, buffalo head, moose head. He was forty-eight years old, tall and pigeon-toed, with a florid complexion, heavy lips, black mustache, and loose, floppy cheeks, and he carried his head slightly down, accenting his double chin, as he peered out the tops of his round, owlish spectacles with shifty hazel eyes.

He was partial to diamond rings, although his favorite ring was one set with two large rubies and a number of small diamonds. He liked to dress in matching combinations: gray hat, gray tie flecked with lavender, gray gloves, gray tweed suit, gray silk socks, and a gray handkerchief with handwoven gray and lavender threads around the edges. One of his most memorable ensembles was a white linen suit with a purple hatband, purple necktie, purple breast pocket handkerchief, and purple silk socks.

When he talked, he sputtered, spraying any near him with saliva, so that those who had no kind feeling for him resorted to the obvious joke behind his back, "Here comes Jess. Get out your umbrella."

Before he entered a room, he would fix his tie, pull his vest down smartly, set his cuffs just so, pat down his hair. He was a timid man; tears came to his eyes easily; and he was terribly frightened of firearms.

He had been born in a small town, Washington Court House, Ohio, about thirty miles south of Columbus. His father, a clerk in a dry goods store, died when he was three years old, and his mother married again–both of her husbands were named Smith–to a man who was elected sheriff of Fayette County at a time when sheriffs legally pocketed their fees along with whatever else came their way. As a child, Jess was never short of cash.

When he graduated from high school, a classmate described him this way: "He is a great sport, takes in all the shows, goes to all the hops, and is a ladies' man in general." After working as an apprentice for several years in a dry goods store, he was set up in his own business by his family, and he became known as the town's Beau Brummell, and no social occasion was felt to be complete–no dance, dinner, or christening–until Jess had arrived in his raiment. Women were said to be especially fond of him. He enjoyed fussing over the right choice of clothes for his clients, and he loved gossip.

When he was in his mid-thirties, he fell in love with Roxy Stinson, the beautiful, tall, redheaded, and thrillingly volatile daughter of Mrs. Eldora Stinson, a widow who had moved to town to set up a conservatory of music on the floor above Jess's dry goods store. In time, Jess married Roxy, to the dismay of Jess's mother, who had to move out to a room in the Cherry Hotel on Main Street. After a year and a half–mostly, it was said, because of the trouble Jess's mother made, perhaps because Jess was impotent–Jess and Roxy were divorced. Jess's mother moved back in with her son; and Jess and Roxy resumed their friendship.

In the lobby of the Astor Hotel, Jess turned to greet William Orr and another man who followed behind him. Orr, a slim, well-dressed man in his late thirties, former midwestern newspaperman, former city editor of the New York *Tribune,* and former private secretary to Charles Whitman, the Republican governor of New York, had fallen on hard times when the Democrats took over New York with Al Smith. At the moment, he was between political appointments.

Orr introduced Jess to John Gorini of the Alps Drug Company, a pharmaceutical establishment in Hell's Kitchen. With the recent passage of the Prohibition laws, drug companies were required to obtain special permits in order to buy alcohol for medicinal purposes. Gorini had applied for a permit to the Prohibition director in New York to buy five hundred cases of liquor. For some reason he had been turned down. Then a man unknown to him, a theatrical agent, had phoned to suggest he get in touch with Bill Orr.

And so Bill Orr introduced Gorini to Jess Smith. They did not speak to one another in the hotel lobby. No money passed between them. They shook hands, Jess returned to his conversation, and the others went their way.

II.

The Little Green House on K Street

ACCORDING TO THE butler, Jess Smith called two or three times a week at the greenstone Victorian townhouse, with the little magnolia bush in the front yard, on K Street in Washington. When Smith arrived, he would go directly to a room where he could confer privately with Howard Mannington, a political acquaintance from Columbus, Ohio.

Mannington, who had handled some of the smaller campaign funds during the recent presidential election, had arrived recently in Washington—seen off at the train station in Ohio by a friend who said, "You ought to be in a position to get pretty much anything through down there, if it's right."

"Hell!" said Mannington, "If it's *right,* they won't need me."

In his late forties, jowly, square-headed, heavy-lidded, thick-lipped with a pug nose, Mannington dressed impeccably, if less noticeably than Jess Smith. He was partial to well-tailored suits, a walnut walking stick, and a tiepin of diamonds and sapphires.

He had worked for a coal company and a power company, and had eased his way into statehouse politics in Columbus, serving for a time as an assistant secretary of state of Ohio, and as a member of the Ohio Railroad Commission. He was known as a smooth talker, convivial, and, in a general way, as a man "to see." He had no official appointment in Washington. When asked what he was doing in the capital, he would smile disarmingly and explain that he was there "to help the attorney general."

From time to time, liquor was delivered to the house twenty cases at a time in a Wells Fargo Express Company truck accompanied by a revenue man carrying a badge and a revolver, and the gossips told of wonderful parties, such as the one–no doubt imaginary–in which a woman was killed with the slivers of a shattered champagne glass thrown at her by another woman.

It was–this much is true–at the little green house on K Street that the money that Gorini gave to an associate of Bill Orr's, who gave it to Bill Orr, was given to Howard Mannington who, in turn, gave Bill Orr the official permits to take back to his acquaintances in New York. The permits cost the liquor dealers $15 apiece. One permit freed one case (three gallons) of liquor. The $15 was for the permit alone. The liquor itself cost extra. Everyone took a cut of the $15: Orr, Mannington, even Gorini took a $1 kickback.

From Chicago, the money came in through H. P. Kraffmiller. From Marietta, Ohio, the money came through Fred Caskey. From elsewhere, the money came in through the constant stream of visitors to the House of Mirth on K Street. The $15 fee covered permits. If, in spite of having such permits, some business associates ran afoul of some naive local enforcement officer, separate fees might be negotiated for immunity from prosecution, change of venue, pardons, or paroles.

The Prohibition commissioner, who worked out of the Treasury Department and who was responsible for the enforcement of

Prohibition throughout the United States, was Roy Haynes, schoolteacher, editor, and one of the leading "dry" spokesmen in America. Haynes had been mayor of Hillsboro, Ohio, where the temperance movement had begun in 1873, and he was appointed commissioner at the insistence of Wayne B. Wheeler, the leader of the Anti-Saloon League. As it turned out, Haynes's reputation as a man of virtue and integrity did not survive life in Washington for more than a few days. Under his administration, his 1,500 enforcement agents, appointed according to the usages of political patronage, discovered–if they had not already known it–that they could make the equivalent of a year's salary in a month's bribes. Haynes's bureau became known as the nation's finest "training school for bootleggers," and Haynes himself provided Mannington with the permits that Mannington sold.

Gorini's first payment for permits was $50,000. During the next three months, he forwarded another $150,000. He understood, Gorini said, that Orr took a cut, Mannington took a cut, and Jess Smith took a cut. He didn't know where the rest went.

The Safe in the Backyard

GASTON B. MEANS was a large, jolly, ingratiating man, six feet tall and weighing more than two hundred pounds, dimpled and balding, with a round face and a confidential manner, and a twinkle in his eyes that sometimes suggested a glimmer of madness. He worked for the Bureau of Investigation, the forerunner of the FBI, which was being run by William J. Burns of Columbus, Ohio. Means, as a Special Employee, earned seven dollars a day. On that salary, he supported–somehow–his family in a townhouse at 903 16th Street, N.W., with a staff of three servants and a chauffeur for his Cadillac.

The house was, said Means, "peculiarly well located . . . with a front and a rear entrance. A lane ran along back of the yard–wide enough to accommodate the parking of a car. My car stood there always–opposite the back gate. This lane or alley twisted a circuitous route that led within a short block to the Department of Justice."

Means spent most of his time in the basement, which was fitted up with six rooms and a bathroom. The front room was furnished with a mahogany rolltop desk and a swivel chair and two telephones, one confidential, unlisted. Next to the desk was a filing cabinet, to which only Means himself had the key. On the walls were a number of excellent maps, primarily of all the waterfronts of the United States. On one wall was an open fireplace with a white marble mantel–"convenient," Means said, "for burning papers." One room–intentionally dark and disquieting–was set aside as the waiting room; another room was reserved for files; a third, a large and comfortably furnished dining room, could accommodate twenty guests for dinner. The laundry room was equipped with white enamel washtubs–"ideal," said Means, "for ice-packed champagne bottles and liquors and wines." The kitchen was well appointed, with both electric and gas stoves as well as a wood stove.

The backyard, however, was the essential point of interest for Means. "We had a back gate that was as strong as the door of a bank vault. Entering this gate (with special key), one was then inside a steel cage–confronted by another gate, equally as strong and opened only by another special key. All around the yard, extending several feet inside the fence–and above the fence some thirty feet, was placed double iron net work, of fine mesh, but thick and strong as the grating protecting a bank. . . . In summer this high iron grating was camouflaged with vines."

Means spent a good deal of time in the backyard–arranging flowerbeds around the fence, and digging a square hole, several feet wide, in the center of the yard. "After getting down a couple of feet or so, I had a wooden platform built that fitted into this place–with an open space in the center. Then, I dug down and through that center for twenty feet–and I lowered into this twenty-foot-deep hole a terra-cotta pipe about eight inches in diameter.

"That was our bank–our safe deposit vault. . . . I had a small steel box, which I kept lowered into this pipe by a strong rope."

In that safe, Means kept the money that Jess Smith brought to him. "Jess Smith," Means said, "always kept detailed accounts of every transaction. He did this for his own protection and from habits of a lifetime. He had been a merchant. His accounts had to balance every Saturday night. Jess never took a nickel that did not belong to him."

At times, Means had as little as $50,000 in the backyard. At one time, he said, he had as much as $500,000 in the backyard. Altogether, he figured about seven million dollars passed through his hands. From time to time, of course, Jess would make a withdrawal and take some of the money home with him to H Street, to the house where he lived with the attorney general of the United States.

The House on H Street

Harry Micajah Daugherty, age sixty-one, the attorney general, was born across town from Jess Smith's home in Washington Court House, Ohio. He was the older of two boys, whose father died when they were youngsters. Both boys went to work at an early age, encouraged by a mother who was determined that they would make good. Harry worked after school and on Saturdays at a grocery store. "He was so little," his mother said, "he had to stand on a box to reach the cash drawer."

Along the way, Harry took an interest in Jess Smith, who was one of the other fatherless boys in town and twelve years younger than Harry. Daugherty took on young Jess with great sympathy—more as a father than a friend or brother—and advised him, coached him, and helped him get started in his dry goods business.

Harry's younger brother Mally meanwhile went straight into the banking business and came, in time, to own the Washington

Court House bank. Harry himself, after he graduated from Washington Court House High School, went on to the University of Michigan, from which he received a law degree in 1881.

Not long after Harry graduated from law school and returned to Washington Court House, he met Lucy Walker, who had come to town to teach music in the public school. She was said to be the most beautiful girl in town, and when Harry heard her sing "Last Night" and "Love's Old Sweet Song," he began to court her. They were married in 1884, and Daughterty's love for her apparently never weakened or wavered. They had two children, a boy and a girl; the boy grew up to be an alcoholic, and the girl was constantly ill. Daugherty's wife developed crippling arthritis at an early age, and Daugherty spent much of his time and thought caring for her and moving her from home to hospital and back again. By the time Jess and Harry had reached Washington, Jess was spending some of his time taking care of Mrs. Daugherty, too, putting her to bed, carrying her to the window to sit in the sunlight. Daugherty himself complained more and more of his own health and, from time to time, would simply collapse from fatigue.

He started out as a criminal lawyer in Washington Court House, but, soon, he found it best to settle out of court and, then, even better to arrange things ahead of time in the halls of the state legislature in Columbus. He became known as a political lawyer, or fixer, and, to a local railroad construction company, he added a list of corporate clients that included the Ohio State Telephone Company, Armour and Company, and the American Tobacco Company.

As a young attorney, he seemed always on the move, always to have a dozen deals in the works. He loved to put things over, but he seemed almost not to care whether he won or lost. He was entirely ruthless; but he carried almost no grudges. He swore copiously, and he often befuddled his less nimble-witted associates with his oblique jests. When the occasion called for it, no one could be more direct. He lied often, flatly, and without shame, to close friends as well as to strangers. He was a shrewd judge of character, adept particularly at seeing another man's weakness.

He first ran for political office in the Fourth Ward of Columbus, a constituency of about a thousand persons, and was elected councilman. He next ran for prosecuting attorney of Fayette County and was elected. He then ran for representative in the state legislature, and he was elected, and reelected. He was never elected to office again.

Soon after he was elected for his second term in the state legislature, he was accused of accepting a bribe of "seven crisp $500 bills" for his vote–this in the days when state legislatures elected United States senators–in a Senate election. Although nothing was ever proven, the accusation began a string of charges, investigations, hearings, inquiries, and trials that accompanied Daugherty all his life. He faced every charge, he met every accusation, he was never convicted of a single crime. But he was never trusted by the voters. He lost elections for nearly every office available in Ohio; he lost twice in campaigns for Congress, once in a campaign for the nomination for state attorney general, once for the nomination for Republican governor, and once for the nomination for United States senator. Not even the politicians trusted him–or perhaps the politicians least of all–and he was defeated, also, for a plethora of other, minor offices.

In the 1920 election, although few politicians liked having him around, and almost none would make a firm deal with him, he threw himself into the presidential campaign with all the swagger, profanity, and robustiousness he could muster. He turned himself into a campaign manager for a dark horse candidate who held back for so long that no one else thought there was a campaign to manage; and, when the Republicans won in November, he found himself, by his own estimation, the leading contender for the office of attorney general. No one knew better, after all, where the bodies were buried, where the finances had come from, where the statutes had been broken, and which lawsuits might need to be settled out of court.

His eyes were disconcerting: one was brown, the other blue. The brown eye had an opaque cast to it, and the blue one was in constant movement, rarely meeting another's eyes directly, but rather circling around whomever he was talking to, as though getting an impression of the other from a psychic aura, or from the atmosphere. With his Wheeling stogy, his pearl stickpin, his round, smooth face–hair parted in the middle–and his thick neck and stocky midsection, he impressed people in Washington as a tough, professional pol. He looked more like the accomplished manipulator, the fellow who never made a false move, than in fact he was.

In the house on H Street, Daugherty and Smith set up an establishment that cost them–so Jess bragged, at least, in a letter to Roxy–$50,000 a year to maintain. They employed a black butler, Walter De Marquis Miller, and an aged cook named Emma Parker, and they received between 50 and 500 visitors a day, at breakfast, lunch, dinner, and late into the evening–congressmen and lobbyists, Ohioans by the carload, men looking for appointments and paroles, pardons and opportunities. "The love nest," Daugherty called it. Will Hays, chairman of the National Republican party and dispenser of political patronage as postmaster general, was often there. Richard Washburn Child paid a courtesy call before he was appointed ambassador to Italy. William J. Burns checked in just before he was appointed director of the Bureau of Investigation. Bill Orr brought the liquor in suitcases. John Ringling stopped by to talk about the arrangements for pitching his circus tents in Pittsburgh. Armour and Company delivered free hams and bacons to the house, and J. Ogden Armour himself stopped by once in a while. Harry Sinclair, the oilman, came by often.

In Daugherty's term as attorney general, he was privileged to pass on the appointment of 88 judges across the United States, circuit, district, and Supreme Court judges, from Hawaii to Maine, from Alaska to Puerto Rico. Those who called on Daugherty and Smith could not be blamed–nor could Daugherty and Smith–for jumping to the conclusion that, in some places at least, the fix was in.

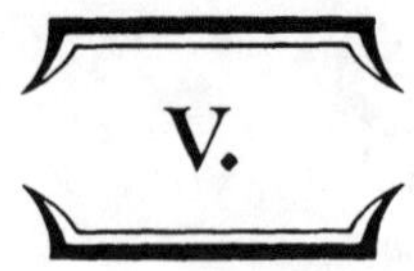

V.

The Poker Party

A LOT OF different fellows sat in on the poker games around the dining room table at the little house on H Street—some smoked cigars, some chewed, most shed their jackets, loosened their ties, undid their collar buttons, partook of the whisky that had been set out by the butler, and made themselves at home.

Ed Scobey, the former sheriff of Pickaway County, Ohio, a beefy fellow whose mouth turned down at the corners, now the director of the United States Mint, was one of the regulars at the table. He must have been relieved to take off his jacket: he looked like a man who had never before been accustomed to buttoning it.

Dick Crissinger, short, with a bow tie, erect and anxious—who had been the head of a small bank in Marion, Ohio, for a few months, was now the comptroller of the currency, and would soon be the governor of the Federal Reserve System—was another of the regulars.

Charlie Forbes often sat in. A "pursy, rufous, convivial, highly energized individual," according to one of his contemporaries, "full of snappy stories and insinuating gossip, boisterous in mirth and fellowship . . . popular with men and alluring to women," Forbes was, as head of the Veterans' Bureau, in charge of disposing of millions of dollars worth of postwar government surplus stocks of sheets, towels, pajamas, rolls of gauze, soap, trucks, and floor wax. He both bought and sold, in order to get rid of surpluses and to make certain that veterans' hospitals were properly stocked. Sometimes he did both at the same time. Even as he sat holding his cards at the poker table, sheets he had purchased at an inflated cost from a friend who gave him a kickback were being brought in one door of a government warehouse–and taken out the other door to be sold cheaply as government surplus to another friend who gave Forbes a kickback.

Thomas W. Miller, who often sat at the table, was the head of the Alien Property Bureau, charged with seeing to the disposition, among other things, of the assets seized during World War I from Germans. Miller had control of 31,000 trusts and several thousand pieces of real estate. An eminently respectable man, a member of Philadelphia's Union League Club and the Bankers of America, Miller was about to work a deal on a German claim on shares of American Metal Company that would net $50,000 for himself, $112,000 for one of the Republican national committeemen, and $224,000 for Jess Smith.

Jap Muma, from Cincinnati, was making a deal to run some contraband prize fight films across state lines. Thomas B. Felder, an old law associate of Daugherty's, had established himself as the attorney to see in New York for any problems with Prohibition enforcement officers. From time to time, Will Hays would stop by, as would Charlie Schwab, head of Bethlehem Steel and interested in the shipping business among other things, and Albert Fall, former senator from New Mexico, and now secretary of the interior.

Ned McLean often joined the game. The house on H Street belonged to him, and he had loaned it to Daugherty and Smith.

McLean was the son of John R. McLean, owner of the Cincinnati *Enquirer,* a figure in Ohio and national politics, owner of a gas company, a street railway, a bank, and a trust company, and owner of the Washington *Post.* Ned, who had inherited none of his father's forcefulness, never quite found a suitable occupation for himself. By the time he was twenty-two, his hands shook so much that he sometimes had to use a sling to get a drink to his lips. He met and married a sharp-witted and rich young woman named Evalyn Walsh, who also had a terrible taste for alcohol, and by the time they had financed the first days of their marriage and their honeymoon abroad, the two had spent $200,000. On their next trip to Europe, evidently overcome by sudden whim, and against the advice of the superstitious Cartier, they bought the cursed Hope Diamond. By 1921, Ned and Evalyn had become idle Washington socialites, and Ned was profoundly grateful to Harry Daugherty for finally giving him a real job: at a salary of a dollar a year, Ned was appointed a special agent of the Department of Justice and given his own badge and secret code number.

Occasionally, too, as often as once a week, and sometimes more often, the poker players would open up their circle to take in one of the most compulsive cardplayers ever to pass through Washington, a man who loved not only to play the game, but to pile side bet upon side bet, who had a couple of poker games every week in his own quarters and then would go out on other nights to one friend's house or another, playing for stakes of money, sets of dishes, or jewelry: the president of the United States, Warren G. Harding, of Marion, Ohio, who arrived, of course, in a limousine, accompanied by his wife, the Duchess, and secret service agents, shed his jacket, rolled up his sleeves, bit off a chew of tobacco (offering the plug cordially to the others around the table), and played the others to exhaustion.

He was a handsome man, genial, gentle, with a warm, resonant, rich voice, a courteous, considerate manner, a man who moved with ease and suppleness, a man with great presence, with a high forehead and distinguished gray hair, and a face that wrinkled into reassuring, paternal smile lines with gratifying frequency; he was calm and contained, solid, forthright, honest, almost noble in bearing, the one man in the group–everyone agreed–who looked like a president.

One evening, one of the other players admired a pearl stickpin the president was wearing, and figured it must have been worth at least four or five thousand dollars.

"I haven't often seen as fine a one," the fellow said.

"Won it at the poker game Wednesday night," said Harding.

"You must have been holding 'em."

"Not so good," said the president. "I got this spading [betting one hand will have a higher spade than another hand] with the man on my left. He took it out of his pocket and said, 'I'll put this up against a hundred dollars.' It looked good to me, so I took him up. I won with a four of spades."

The fellow was impressed–especially impressed by the odds that the unknown man to the president's left had given to Harding: 40 or 50 to 1. But, where Harding came from, such long odds were not uncommon. Indeed, sitting down at the poker table and letting another fellow come out ahead from time to time was the old, traditional way of passing money in Ohio politics.

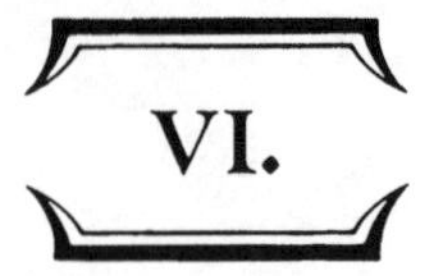

VI.

Warren Harding's Baby Pictures

WARREN GAMALIEL HARDING—born on November 2, 1865, in Blooming Grove, a tiny farm village in the green rolling countryside of northern Ohio—was a beautiful baby. He looked like a little girl, and, even years later, after he had grown into a substantial-seeming man, he had a mincing, prancing step.

The boy's father, George Tryon Harding, was a small, idle, shiftless, impractical, lazy, daydreaming, catnapping fellow whose eye was always on the main chance. He started out to be a schoolteacher—an easy sort of profession, it seemed at the time—but soon became bored with that. He bought a secondhand set of medical books, swotted up some medical knowledge, followed a doctor on his country rounds, and after spending two terms at the Western College of Homeopathy in Cleveland, was a doctor—a dignified sort of profession, although he never built up much of a practice, and he spent a lot of time napping on his own moth-eaten examining

The country doctor, George Tryon Harding, Warren's father, sets out in his buggy.

room couch. His love was aroused not by medicine but by swapping: he was always eager to make a trade, a trade in horses, cows, pieces of machinery, bits of land, farm tools. He would trade with anyone for anything–although, on the whole, he hardly ever traded up, and, after a lifetime of deals, of many good and bad swaps, hard times and lucky breaks, of loans and handouts, bailouts and family welfare, he ended up slightly less than even.

Her hair pulled tightly back, her eyes calm and gentle, Warren's mother, Phoebe Harding, was both austere and lovely.

The boy's mother, Phoebe, was a devout churchgoer who attended the Methodist church every day, took her family to every Sunday service and church supper that the Methodists held, hummed hymns as she did her housework, and quoted Scripture with almost every remark she made. She worked hard, keeping a well-ordered house, cooking, baking, giving birth to eight children, and working as a professional midwife. She had a taste for the finer things: she taught Warren the alphabet, working with a stick of charred wood on the bottom of a shoebox, and set him to memorizing poems of refined sentiments before he was four years old. When the boy went visiting with his parents, he would turn to his mother and ask, "Will it be all right for me to speak my piece

Harding's birthplace, near Blooming Grove, Ohio, was a plain frame farmhouse with a well in the side yard. The house stood atop a knoll that overlooked rolling countryside as rich and green as the eighteenth fairway at Burning Tree country club.

now?" And, upon receiving his mother's permission, he would deliver his piece without hesitation. She herself spoke in a quiet voice, firmly, always with love for her son, and always with complete conviction that he would succeed in whatever he set out to do. When he was older, Warren took flowers to his mother every Sunday morning–or, when he was out of town, made certain the local florist got them to her–without fail, until she died.

The boy, Warren, spent his life uncertainly suspended between the character of his father and that of his mother. When he relaxed, he tended to be like his father; like his father, he often thought he could acquire something better than he had–a deal, a job, a wife; but he could never give up, either, his hope of being, himself, someone better than he was.

VII.

The Little Nigger

HIS SCHOOLMATES CALLED him a "little nigger." He had dark hair and a dark complexion, and the rumor was that his great-great-grandfather Amos had been a West Indian black or that some other member of the family had been a mulatto, and Warren could not be sure.

Although he denied it, he could not get over the taunting and whispering. Marked from birth as an outsider, he spent his life trying to get in, to blend with the crowd. Whatever complexities of character may have played through him, he smoothed them over, repressed or hid them. He was just another country boy: he swam in the creek, he played sandlot baseball, he painted barns and houses, he milked cows and curried horses. He was always noticed as a boy who was kind to others, who did not believe in name calling, and who was charitable to those who were different or somehow flawed.

He attended a one-room schoolhouse in Blooming Grove and memorized passages from the *McGuffey Eclectic Readers,* and although he seemed to make no special effort at his studies, it was clear that he was smarter than his schoolmates. When his father moved the family to a little yellow house in nearby Caledonia, Warren distinguished himself there in school as someone who was good at spelling long words and who (after those years of nurturing by his mother) "shone at recitations." But his dilemma—to stand out, and at the same time to blend in—held him in a particularly tight grip.

His first chance to resolve the dilemma occurred when his father brought home a B-flat cornet one day. Warren's father had acquired it in one of his trades. Warren, age ten, was taught to play by a local harness maker, and soon Warren was good enough to join the Caledonia Aeolian Band, which held forth in the local bandstand on Saturday nights and occasionally played a stint in a neighboring town. Harding, said one of his boyhood chums, "could execute No. 24 in the Black Book with personal sangfroid and astonishing musical force. Barring the bass drummer, no other member of the band could make as much noise."

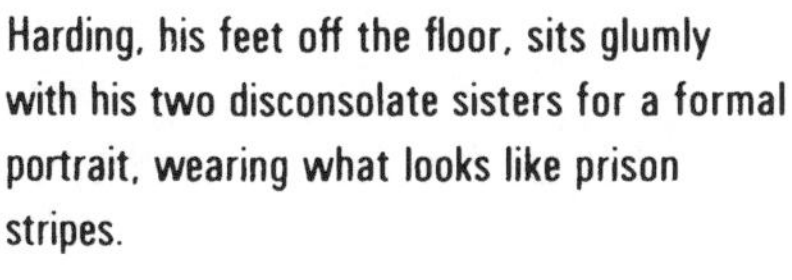

Harding, his feet off the floor, sits glumly with his two disconsolate sisters for a formal portrait, wearing what looks like prison stripes.

VIII.

The Happy Booster

In the summer of 1875, when Warren was still ten, his father made a keen trade and acquired the ownership of the town's down-and-out newspaper, the *Caledonia Argus,* a journal that appeared whenever its editor was able to scrape together enough money to buy some paper. The editor, Will Warner, who was also the paper's publisher, reporter, typesetter, distributor, and janitor, was kept on the job by Warren's father, and Warren and a friend went in to the newspaper office to help. Will Warner wore a top hat at work and must have looked like an eccentric scarecrow: he was a vision that Harding never forgot. Warren swept the floor, delivered papers, washed down the press, and returned bits of type to the type tray, and occasionally he was allowed to set some type himself and help to print up a page of the paper. Will Warner gave Warren a makeup rule, a tiny steel ruler, about two-and-a-half inches long, and Harding kept it as a lucky piece—his only such talisman—for the rest of his life.

The makeup rule was a memento of his first "grown-up" job (even, to be sure, despite its lamentably modest size, a symbol of manhood); it was a reminder of Will Warner, a man who did not fear to stand out in his top hat; it was a reminder of all of those values of the small-town newspaper—its boosting, neighborly, cheerful, good news, family-praising, commerce-plugging principles that gave Harding, finally, a way to promote himself by promoting others, to stand out without asserting himself.

When Harding was fourteen, he went off to nearby Iberia College. Fourteen was not an unusually young age to begin a college career at the time, although not all young Ohio boys aspired to such intellectual heights. The college had a teaching faculty of three—two clergymen and a professor of ancient languages, and Harding graduated—as one of his boyhood chums said, taking the edge off Harding's distinction as a college man—either "first or second in his class," since there were only two graduates from the college that year.

He drifted then, like his father, alarmingly. He returned home—his father had moved the family once more, this time a few miles west, to Marion, the county seat—and Warren taught school there for a term and then abandoned it. His father picked up some old lawbooks in a trade, and Harding read those for a while, with the thought of becoming a lawyer, but then gave up on that. Nothing felt quite right to him. He took a job as an insurance salesman for a short time, but he made a mistake in his calculations, sold policies at the wrong rate, became discouraged, and quit.

He had a talent for words, and he enjoyed playing with his talent. "Hasn't it been wet and slippery," he wrote to an aunt at the time he was teaching school. "The ice facilitated falling and all seemed to embrace—the opportunity of an easy fall. One morning I saw several new constellations when on my way to educational headquarters but, they soon disappeared only to be seen by a similar fall. The floods, however, did not effect the Marionites to any ex-

tent. How is Uncle Dan, Mother, Grandma'am, and the rest of the relatives? I am coming up when school closes then I will visit all, Gert included PERHAPS. How does Cass sail forth? Stingy as ever, I suppose. Does he 'mash'?"

He had a good mind, but not a great one, and it had little to work on, so that it became lazy and merely facile. Harding's real genius lay in ingratiating himself with people, and that was a talent that he practiced constantly, on everyone, male and female, up and down the social scale, friend and stranger, until he was perhaps the most ingratiating man in America.

He took to hanging around the local livery stable and the courthouse. He lifted the occasional glass in a bar, and he paid occasional visits to the town's whorehouses. He took up playing poker on Saturday nights. Above all, he liked to talk, to pass the time of day, to exchange pleasantries, to idle away the hours dis-

A substantial edifice, this solid brick building was taken over to house the offices of the Marion *Star* when Harding's newspaper became well established.

cussing politics; *bloviating,* he called it. But no job suited him exactly. Nothing fit his needs quite as perfectly as newspapering.

In the spring of 1884, his father acquired another newspaper—putting up his interest in a house lot (that he had got in another trade) in exchange for a half-interest in a dying local paper, the Marion *Star.* Warren moved in with the august title of editor; but his stint was cut short when a lien was placed against the house lot that his father had put up for the paper.

When it looked as though Warren would turn to full-time bloviating again, his father arranged for him to take a job with Colonel James Vaughan, who ran another paper in Marion, the *Mirror.* Warren worked as a reporter, ad salesman, and delivery boy, but not for long. Vaughan fired him for loafing and for spending too much time hanging around the local Republican party headquarters. Vaughan was a Democrat.

Soon after Warren was fired, two of his old pals from the Caledonia Aeolian Band appeared in Marion—Jack Warwick and Johnnie Sickle. The three young men decided to get together and buy back the Marion *Star.* They figured they could get it for $300. Johnnie Sickle had just inherited $1,600; he put up his $100. Jack Warwick, who had no money, borrowed $100 from Sickle. Warren went to Colonel Vaughan and convinced the colonel that a revived Marion *Star* would be a fine nuisance for the colonel's only competitor in Marion, the Republican *Independent.*

They started with nothing, setting their own type, writing and editing and selling ads and delivering copies door to door, juggling the books, keeping one step ahead of the sheriff to avoid one lien or another. Their editorial policy was simple and straightforward: "to boom Marion and Marion men against all outsiders," Jack Warwick said. "Every enterprise was given all the attention the traffic would bear. . . . We exploited railroads that never got beyond the blueprint and we saw smoke rolling out of the chimneys of factories before the excavations were made for the foundations."

If he possibly could, Harding kept unpleasant stories out of his paper. He wanted to be an agreeable neighbor, and he wanted, too, to avoid making things any harder for men "whose weaknesses got them into trouble."

"Jack," he said one day to Warwick, "I wish we could cut out all police court news."

"First," Warwick said, "do away with the police court then."

"Of course, that can't be done, but some day I hope to keep such stuff out of the paper. In the meantime we can disregard much of it and minimize the rest."

Marion was a town of about five thousand in population. It had been a market town and then a grain center, trading on the surrounding fields of corn and alfalfa that began just at the edge of town. With the coming of the railroad, the town acquired some industries as well. Edward Huber, for instance, had arrived in Marion the year that Harding was born, and had begun to manufacture hayrakes. Within twenty years, he was making an array of farm tools and a patented threshing machine and had formed a new company with a young fellow who had invented a steam shovel. By the time Harding was publishing the *Star,* the Huber Manufacturing Company had more than seventy employees and sold a million dollars worth of machinery every year.

The town grew, and Harding's newspaper grew with it, partly because of Harding's hard work and his editorial policy of flattering Marion, and partly because everything flourished in Marion in those days. New residential streets cropped up with fine new homes, the finest of them large wooden American castles with broad front porches, verandahs, swings and railings, lawns that rolled on continuously from one house to the next in neighborly openness. Marion soon had a new Baptist church, a new music hall, a new jail, new businesses and opportunities of every kind that Harding celebrated in the *Star.*

The editor, in rumpled suit and worn shoes, reposes at his desk in the *Star* offices, with telephone for bloviating close at hand.

Their office was on the second floor of an old building in the center of town, and Harding could walk every morning from his family's run-down house in a shabby section of town to his office, saying hello to those he met along the way, greeting them by first name, finding out about new babies, businesses, gossip, and schemes. The *Star*'s office had been an old job-printing shop, and along with the name of the paper and five hundred subscribers who were casual about paying their ten cents a week subscription money, Harding and his partners took over a thirdhand, manually operated Fairhaven press, and enough type to set a few pages of news before breaking up the printing forms, redistributing the type, and setting a few more pages. "At distributing type," Warwick said of Harding, "he was not up to the average journeyman, but at distributing ink he was a star of the first magnitude. He loved ink to the point of taking it unto his bosom."

Harding's own office sported a brass cuspidor on top of his desk, and he felt so at home in the office that he sometimes spent the night. Some of the help, itinerant printers, newsboys, and others spent the night sometimes, too. In time, Harding and his partners were able to afford a large new counter in the offices, where they could receive people who wanted to come in to place ads in the newspaper. "The new counter," Warwick said, ". . . soon justified itself. Though never crowded by day, it was at times crushed to its capacity by night, being long enough only for two to sleep on comfortably."

The boys in the office called him W.G., and he dropped into the newsroom and pressroom, such as they were, frequently, even after the enterprise was so prosperous that he and his Caledonia pals no longer did all the work themselves. He might ask who had a plug of tobacco, and bite off a chaw. Once, when the boys in the pressroom were short of tobacco, W.G. went out, got a plug, returned a few minutes later, and nailed the plug to the wall for all to cut off a slice whenever the need came on. He loved the printing press and the type; he enjoyed the companionship of his cronies; he took a paternal interest in the newsboys; he loved to put his feet on his desk, look out the window, and pass the time bloviating.

He had a weakness for tramp printers, who would drift into Marion, set type for a while, sleep in the *Star* offices, and then wander on. He seemed, Warwick said, "thoroughly to understand these irresponsible, carefree wanderers. To him the hidden treasures of their souls were revealed and he saw them not as tramp printers, but as men capable of human emotions"–as his mother understood his father, or should have. Among the tramp printers who stood out among the rest was Colonel Hargot. "Tall and dignified, he always wore a high silk hat that was the worse for wear and a Prince Albert coat. The colonel was one who didn't like work, but he liked Warren G. because Warren G.'s clothes fitted Colonel Hargot. The colonel carried a cane to show that the world owed him a living." One of the others who came and went was Shorty Johnson, and when Shorty appeared in town after some brief or lengthy absence, he would invariably step into the *Star* office with the cheerful, ever-hopeful salutation: "How are you fixed?" Another of the old regulars was a Civil War veteran who always bedded down in a pile of old newspapers and, by way of bidding good-night, would say, "Wake me up when Kirby dies"–whoever that had been.

Harding was never heard to shout, or even to raise his voice, certainly not to throw a temper tantrum. His self-control was so complete as to seem entirely natural. His pals and colleagues took him as one of the boys, and he was enormously popular. He was not, however, without ambition. He allowed a grumbling difference of opinion with Sickle to fester until Sickle threw in his hand and moved out West; and he won Warwick's interest in the *Star* in a game of poker–a loss that the easygoing Warwick never held against Harding, or let get in his way of staying on as an employee. "He was one of us," Warwick said, "and he insisted that we worked 'with him' not 'for him.'" But, henceforth, Harding owned the paper.

The Perfect Marriage

He married the daughter of the richest man in town—which showed something both of his father's urge to trade up, and his mother's sense of the finer things. Florence Kling was the daughter of Amos Kling, the town's financier who had begun as a clerk in a hardware store, taken over the business, moved his capital into mortgages and real estate, organized some banks, backed the building of the brand-new Marion Hotel, which cost $30,000, and become the richest man in Marion. He opposed his daughter's marriage to Harding. Indeed, when he met Harding at the courthouse one day, he cursed out his daughter's fiancé and called him a nigger. Amos did not attend the wedding, and he did not visit the young couple's house until twenty-two years later.

Florence's mother was Louisa Bouton of New Canaan, Connecticut, who could trace her ancestry back to a distinguished family of French Huguenots who landed in America in 1635. Florence had, then, both new money and old distinction in her lineage.

Florence had been married once before to Pete DeWolfe, the scion of an even more distinguished family, by Marion standards, than the Klings—the DeWolfe's being an "older" family and the proprietors of the local coal yard. Florence and Pete had a son, who grew up, after his parents' divorce, in the home of his Kling grandparents, neglected by his mother. He died at the age of thirty-five of alcoholism.

Amos had evidently wanted his daughter to be a boy, and Florence grew into a hardheaded, awkward, somewhat ungainly young woman, strong willed and dominating. Jack Warwick said that one day when she was horseback riding her mount started to buck and rear—frightening the men who stood helplessly nearby. She battled the horse until, at last, both horse and rider toppled over to the ground. Warwick said that as the horse went over, "the rider slipped to the ground and when the animal was prostrate, caught him by the bridle, pinned his head to the ground, and sat on it until the fiery steed had time to give his better instincts a chance to work."

Some years later, one of Florence's secretaries said that her "well-kept hands were a speaking index to her character. They were unusually large, strong, powerful, crushing, indicating ability to firmly grasp and capacity to overcome all obstacles. In appearance her hands did not fit her delicate body. This incongruity was illustrative of a further disparity; she had the dominant, driving brain of a strong man, and the exquisite, frail body of the gentlewoman."

Strong but delicate, powerful but frail, domineering but often ill, she had very beautiful, alert blue eyes. She moved quickly; she was energetic, clear minded, purposeful, and decisive. Harding called her "the Duchess," and she had those qualities, too, of a slight haughtiness, a sense of deserved superiority, of the right to be demanding, of a somewhat chilly nature, the person beyond whom there was no further appeal.

She was the perfect match for him: she was five years older

Florence Harding, with buckles on her shoes, a print dress, and neatly marcelled hair, gazes directly at the photographer. (Ohio Historical Society)

than Harding, and she had the fierce loyalty to "her Warren," and the pride that his mother had. She expected him to succeed, and like his mother, she held him firmly to the high standards that would bring success, money, recognition. He needed her, or felt he did, to keep himself from backsliding, laziness, shiftlessness, whim. When it came to taking a wife, he had chosen well, and he knew it.

Immediately following the wedding, Harding was overcome by fits of indigestion that were so severe and so impossible to assuage that he was compelled, by the end of the year, to go to the health sanitarium at Battle Creek, Michigan, for two months. After his rest cure, he returned to his bride–and was overcome once more by chronic indigestion that was so painful and relentless that he had to return to Battle Creek for fully five months. Following this second session at Battle Creek, he was able to return home and stay there–although, from time to time, he would have to go back to Battle Creek for respite, and he never, for the rest of his life, fully overcame his indigestion.

A Short Course in Political Science

"IF YOU WANT to get along," the one-time Speaker of the House of Representatives, Sam Rayburn, said, "go along." When Harding was only twenty-two years old, he set out for the state Republican convention as a delegate from Marion fully expecting to be a success in this as he had been in every other endeavor. As a Marion booster, and a Republican booster, and a newspaperman, it was only natural that he be brought along to the convention, and he proved himself an agreeable, likeable young fellow, a loyal supporter of the Republican party, of Ohio, and of America–and willing to speak out in favor of any of these causes at picnics or women's clubs, barbecues or meetings of the Elks' club.

Because he was a loyal party man he was happy to run for county auditor in the late 1880s, although there was no chance of a Republican winning in that particular election–and, after a decade of similar unselfish services to the party, accepting defeat cheerfully,

The Capitol Building in Columbus, Ohio, provided the classrooms and the playing fields of the Tafts, for Harding, for Fire Engine Joe Foraker and for Boss Cox, and for more federal jobholders than any other state gave the nation. (The Bettmann Archive, Inc.)

like a good soldier, he was given the Republican nomination for the Ohio State Senate in 1898, and won.

Ohio politics was a rats' nest of warring factions–but Harding amiably declined to take sides. He promoted everyone's cause, doing favors equally for the Cincinnati faction and the Cleveland faction, for the boys of Columbus as well as for the legislators from rural districts. "There may be an abler man in the Senate than Harding," the governor said, "but when I want things done I go to him."

He was on his way to becoming a politician's politician–infinitely loyal, patient, self-effacing, conciliatory, willing to be of use, flexible, tolerant of frailty and foible, fitting in, going along. By 1903, there was already talk of running Harding for governor, although, when the bosses favored Myron Herrick, Harding remained as equable and affable as ever. He said contentedly that, if the party elders favored Herrick, then he thought Herrick would be nominated at the convention "by acclamation." His cheerful acquiescence might almost have seemed simple minded, had he not put himself forward modestly–almost unnoticeably–as a possible candidate for lieutenant governor. He was given the nomination–the office was and is, as such things go, a minor one–and he and Herrick won.

The rewards for a political career in Ohio could be substantial, and any young man who had gotten along as Harding had might well have entertained even greater ambitions. Because Ohio was such a politically active, and corrupt, state–with such gutter fighters as Boss George Cox and Fire Engine Joe Foraker of Cincinnati; such hard money arm twisters as Mark Hanna, the Red Boss of Cleveland; and such snooty patricians as Charlie and William Howard Taft–anyone who came up through Ohio politics was destined to have a first-rate education in the intricacies and pitfalls of forcing and scuttling legislation, manipulating conventions, rigging elections, securing campaign contributions from large and small corporations, disposing of public funds, and letting utility franchises, road contracts, permits, licenses, and jobs. In the period between the end of the Civil War and World War I, Ohio provided more federal jobholders and cabinet members than any other state in the Union. So well schooled, and so skilled, were Ohio politicians that, in the same period, Ohio provided seven out of the twelve presidents of the United States–or every single Republican president except two, who succeeded to the job from the vice-presidency.

They said they were elected because Ohio was in the middle of the country, and because Ohio was the crossroads of the country, a unique blend of North and South, East and West, of industrialists and farmers, old settlers and new frontiersmen. But that was just convention blather. The truth was that Ohio politicians did well because the state weeded out all but the most ferocious survivors, and the survivors built a network over the years that went from Cincinnati to Washington and back again.

In 1905, Harding reached for the nomination for governor of Ohio, and he was slapped down. He had been too hasty. He had forgotten loyalty: Herrick himself wanted to run again for governor. Although it was clear that he could not possibly win the election, loyalty decreed that he must be given the nomination. He was, and he lost, and Harding returned to his office at the Marion *Star* to spend several years remembering to remember to go along. This is the first and last principle of party politics, and once Harding got it firmly fixed in his mind he needed no other principle.

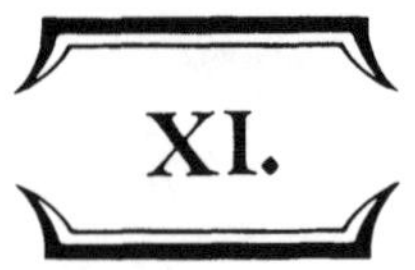

XI.

A Close Call

THE MOMENT WAS irresistible. The Duchess had had major surgery for a kidney ailment and required a long period of convalescence. Harding's friend Jim Phillips, the co-owner of a dry goods store on Center Street, felt ill and out of sorts, so he went off, at Harding's recommendation, to the Battle Creek sanitarium. Harding himself, stung by his failed attempt to snatch the governorship, was in need of solace and reassurance.

Carrie Phillips, Jim's wife, was thirty years old at the time, nine years younger than Harding, a beautiful young woman with golden hair, a round, pretty face, a full womanly figure, and a slender waist; she was warm and sensual, with quick, sometimes unpredictable passions, an exciting woman, an emotional adventure that might lead anywhere, a young woman full of wishes about the world beyond Marion, full of dreams, and, above all, full of a thousand ardent passions. She had an eight-year-old daughter, and she had just lost a five-year-old son—a loss from which she could not recover, for which she needed profound consolation.

Harding fell in love with her as he had never fallen in love with anyone else. They made love at Carrie's house on South Main Street, and when they were apart, whether for a day or, because of business or the need for discretion, for a week, Harding wrote letters to her, letters filled with an outpouring of longing, of craving, of languishing, of lingering soliloquies of his wishes to caress and kiss her, of frank descriptions of his yearning for her lips and breasts, of extravagant happy praise of her eyes, the sound of her voice, her hair, her jokes, her murmurings, her thoughts of the world, her whispers, her dresses, her cheekbones, her earlobes, her laughter, her songs, the touch of her hand, her thighs, her shoulder, the nape of her neck, her flirtatiousness, her warmth and her loveliness.

His letters ran to thirty and forty pages. Sometimes he threw in a terrible piece of doggerel, sometimes romantic verse, sometimes rhymed jokes. His letters were mostly awkward things, full of passages that would make any voyeur squirm and blush in embarrassment for their clumsiness, their desperate sentimentality, their inability, finally, to express all that was in Harding's heart. They are the letters of a man who had spent his life hiding his feelings, not revealing them, who had never had any practice writing love letters or speaking of such intimate things, and so hardly knew what to do when he came to want to express his deepest feelings, and to tell the truth.*

He was a handsome man—with a fleck of gray at the temples by this time—a man of boundless energy and cheerfulness, with an expansive smile and a ready handshake, the sort of man who infused everyone he met with a feeling of happiness and security. A teenage schoolgirl who saw one of his campaign posters at about this time fell in love with him at first sight—overcome as she later

* The letters are now, because of litigation by Harding's heirs, sealed by court order. They may not be quoted directly—or even seen (so I am told)—except in clandestinely circulated, purloined copies.

recalled, with "unforgettable sensations," knowing at once "that he was for me my 'ideal American.' "

The teenage girl cut out pictures of him from the newspapers and put them on her bedroom wall, as though he might be a teenage idol—someone who radiated excitement, someone destined for brilliance in a larger world.

Carrie must have been drawn to him, in part, at least, out of a similar sense of him—for she, too, had an urge to get out of Marion and into a life somehow richer, more exciting, and still secure.

Carrie and Harding carried on their affair for five years—meeting sometimes in another town where Harding had gone to make a political speech. Sometimes, bizarrely, Harding and the Duchess, and Jim and Carrie, would go off together on motoring trips. Once they even managed to go, all of them together, on a month-long holiday to Europe.

Aboard the ship, as they traveled across the Atlantic, after the Duchess and Jim had gone to their staterooms, Harding and Carrie would meet out on the deck, to embrace in the shadows and to talk. Sometimes Carrie, undone by the strain of the situation, would feel herself yielding to Harding's caresses, and then suddenly push him away.

Letters home, to friends in Marion, show a man resolutely uncomplicated, resolutely bland, resolutely optimistic, resolutely able to ride right through any situation with perfect equanimity.

"Saturday," Harding wrote home to a friend, "we stopped at Madeira, drank of the wine, bought of the embroideries, and sent a wave of prosperity over the island. Mighty pretty place. I could gladly stay a couple of weeks. Cannot say I greatly like riding on ox-drawn sleds over cobblestone pavements, but we tried it. Made the ascent of one of the mountains by cog-wheel railway and tobaganed [sic] down. Same stunt in another form. The tabog is an iron-shod sled, pulled, pushed, or held back by two Portuguese, and we descended over two miles of paved mountain roads and streets in that sled, with the two poor men pushing, panting, puffing, and pulling. I never gave anybody a fee so willingly in my life."

So what if he seemed to enjoy his own good looks too much, if he was too attentive to his own appearance, too pleased with his own charm, too frequently given to preening, too fond of the words "becoming" and "seemly." So what if his interminable letters to Carrie sometimes conveyed less the sense that he professed his love than that he loved to profess—or even, sometimes, raised the question whether he was trying to talk himself into a feeling he did not feel?

Whatever his failings, however preoccupied, he did work harder at courting Carrie than anyone else ever had, write to her more than any other man ever had, appreciate her more than any other man had, try harder than any other man had to break through the limitations of character and convention that bound him—in order to love her.

Why Harding and Carrie broke up is not entirely clear. It appears that Carrie wanted to marry Harding, and Harding balked. Doubtless he found it hard to consider leaving the Duchess, who held him so firmly to the course he had plotted out for himself, who supported him so completely in what he wanted. Perhaps he found it hard to imagine what would become of him if he began to give in to his feelings—to begin, perhaps, to follow his whims, recklessly, as his father had done.

What is certain is that of all the people Harding surrounded himself with, and kept around him, Carrie was the only one who did not want him to go farther in politics. Politics only took him away from her. Once he understood the choice she offered him, he backed away completely. It had been a close call: he might have fallen in love, and dropped his career.

Carrie, her feelings hurt, commenced to talk of how much she had enjoyed Europe, and especially Germany, and of how she might like to return to live there one day. No one tried to talk her out of it. She began, then, to belittle his political aspirations, and that finished it for him. He began to travel more, to accept more invitations to speak in places where Carrie could not easily accompany him—and she talked more and more of going off to live abroad.

At last, Carrie did take her daughter and go off to settle in Germany. She wrote home–both to her husband and to Harding–to say that she was not coming back. Neither of the men wrote to implore her to change her mind. When she finally did return, it was to her husband.

XII.

The World's Most Exclusive Club

HARDING RENEWED HIS efforts at politics at just the time the Old Guard of the Republican party had come under attack from a reform movement led by the former president of the United States, Teddy Roosevelt, and the Progressives. The bosses feared that a genuine, popular, grass-roots movement of reformers and mere citizens might take control of the party from them. There was plenty of work for a loyal party man, and Harding went out on the speaking circuit again, talking about how everyone was a reformer at heart, how everyone wanted to stand pat when things were fine, and progress when something new was called for, how all Republicans had the same basic interest at heart. Harding had become the country's most practiced champion of harmony, unity, and smoothing things over. By 1912, when President William Howard Taft decided to try to hang onto the presidency for a second term, Harding had performed so loyally that Taft tossed him a bone by asking him to make the nominating speech at the Republican Convention.

Harding, wearing a brand-new cutaway with a red geranium in his buttonhole, understood perfectly the part he had to play. As he stepped up to the speaker's podium, he was greeted by boos, hisses, and catcalls. The bosses were going to railroad Taft through the convention.

The reformers were shocked at the behavior of the bosses. It was clear to everyone that Taft, if nominated, would lose. The reformers could not believe the bosses wanted to put up a losing candidate. It had not occurred to the Progressives that the bosses would far rather lose the election to the Democrats than lose the Republican party to the reformers. The convention was designed to be an elaborate lesson in the principle of party loyalty. Even before Harding began to speak, some of the delegates started to rub pieces of sandpaper together, to sound like a steam engine getting underway–and called out "Toot! Toot! All aboard! Choo! Choo!" Harding, spokesman of the bosses, had become an old hack, even before he had ever quite been a rising star.

Who ruled America, that was the question; and Harding had the answer: the people ruled America, "a plain people and a sane people . . ."

"Where?" a heckler shouted from the audience.

". . . ruling with an unwavering faith and increased confidence in that fine embodiment of honesty, that fearless executor of the law . . ."

At the far end of the hall, a Pennsylvania delegate was knocked to the ground by a solid punch to the nose.

". . . that inspiring personification of courage, that matchless exemplar of justice that . . ."

"Choo! Choo! Choo! Choo!"

". . . that glorious apostle of peace and amity . . ."

Two members of the delegation from South Dakota got into a fist fight.

". . . William Howard Taft!"

"Choo! Choo! Choo! Choo! We want Teddy! We want Teddy!"

"Progress is not proclamation nor palaver. It is not pretense nor play on prejudice. It is not the perturbation of a people passion-wrought, nor a promise proposed."

Delegates started to get up out of their chairs and leave the auditorium. Harding's style of speaking—the old mellifluous, alliterative, nineteenth-century style of the wailing smoothie—was already old-fashioned. He was good at it. He still "shone at recitation." But it was the style of an old pol trying to put one over. There was nothing spontaneous or real about it. For all of its sly references to the issues at hand, it hardly seemed to grapple with any of the issues. To the extent that it was not infuriating, it was boring.

"Progression is everlastingly lifting the standards that marked the end of the world's march yesterday and planting them on new and advanced heights today. Tested by such a standard, President Taft is the greatest Progressive of the age."

The end of the speech brought forth the strained approving shouts of the loyalists, the wild, derisive bellowing of the reformers, and Harding stepped back down from the podium, thoroughly disgraced and victorious.

Taft lost the election, of course, to Woodrow Wilson; and the Progressives, though down, were not out. The Old Guard still needed loyalists to hold the line against the insurgents. And so, in 1914, when it came time to choose a nominee for the office of United States senator from Ohio, the bosses looked around for a dignified and qualified candidate, and no one was better qualified than Harding.

To be favored by the bosses was to be nominated, and to be the Republican nominee was to be elected. Thus, in 1915, Harding suddenly found himself in Washington, a member of the world's most exclusive club.

Both of the Hardings had an uncertain time measuring up to the place their ambitions had brought them. Just as Warren continued to have digestive problems, the Duchess was often ill with one complaint or another. She seemed to dress too well, to have her hair done too often, and too perfectly, and to have acquired an air of grandeur that overshot the mark.

Evalyn Walsh McLean, the wife of the heir to the Washington *Post* fortune, had a certain sympathy for the Duchess and her husband. She met the Hardings for the first time at the home of Alice Roosevelt Longworth – the daughter of Teddy, the wife of the patrician congressman Nicholas Longworth from Ohio. "We had gone there," Evalyn said, "for a poker game. That evening I decided that the new junior senator from Ohio . . . was a stunning man. He chewed tobacco, biting from a plug that he would lend, or borrow, and he did not care if the whole world knew that he wore suspenders. However, whatever Alice cares to say, I say he was not a slob."

As a senator, Harding was exceedingly careful not to stand out. He introduced no legislation that might be construed to be either important or controversial. Altogether, he introduced 134 bills, of which 122 were concerned with local Ohio matters, and the others were addressed to such issues as the celebration of the landing of the Pilgrims. He was careful to establish himself as a man who did not want to make any sort of public record, but rather as a man who was happy to blend in and go along and do his business in private. He was, therefore, an extremely popular senator – judged at once by his peers to be both sound and agreeable, an able senator, reliable, a man to be counted on, mature, above all "reasonable." He was one of the most highly admired members of the Senate; he made friends easily; he kept a flask of Bourbon in his desk; and he was known to be available for golf or poker at any time.

A Girl on His Arm

DURING HIS TERM as senator, Harding received a letter from a Marion girl who had moved to New York City: "I wonder if you will remember me; my father was Dr. Britton, of Marion, Ohio. . . . I have been reading of the imperative demand for stenographers and typists throughout the country. . . ."

Harding did indeed remember her: Nan Britton, the teenage girl who had fallen in love with his campaign posters in 1910, during his ill-fated attempt to take the nomination for governor of Ohio, when she was a fourteen-year-old schoolgirl, and he was forty-four. Her infatuation with the older man had become so problematical that her father had even called on Harding to see, as man to man, whether they could find some way to redirect her impossible feelings.

In her early twenties, she was as insouciant as ever, still with plump cheeks, a flirtatious manner of looking out the corners of her eyes, an ample body, a breathtaking innocence, and a wish simply to throw herself on a man, be told entirely what to do, and be taken care of.

Harding could hardly reply quickly enough. He did remember her, "you may be sure of that, and I remember you most agreeably, too." He mentioned that there was "every probability" of his being in New York the next week and would look her up, that he would "take pleasure in doing it."

> My dear Mr. Harding:
>
> It was good to know that you remembered me; and I appreciate your kind interest and prompt response. . . . I will say frankly that I have had little practical experience. . . . I am hoping that you will be in New York next week and that I can talk with you. . . . There is so much I want to tell you; and I am sure that I could give you a better idea of my ability—or rather the extent of my ability, for it is limited—and you could judge for yourself as to the sort of position I could competently fill.

He phoned her from the Manhattan Hotel, at Madison Avenue and 42nd Street. "He was standing on the steps of the hotel," Nan recalled, "when I reached there." They sat in the hotel lounge and reminisced, touching upon her childhood infatuation with him—"and he seemed immensely pleased that I still retained such feelings. I could not help being perfectly frank."

Some sort of convention was going on in New York at the time, Harding told Nan, and he "confessed that he was obliged to take the one room available in the Manhattan Hotel—the bridal chamber! He asked me to come up there with him so that we might continue our conversation without interruptions or annoyances.

"The bridal chamber of the Manhattan Hotel was, to me, a very lovely room, and . . . we had scarcely closed the door behind us when we shared our first kiss. . . . I shall never, never forget how

Mr. Harding kept saying, after each kiss, "God! . . . God, Nan!' in high diminuendo, nor how he pleaded in tense voice, 'Oh, dearie, tell me it isn't hateful to you to have me kiss you!' "

The bed, said Nan, remained undisturbed. Between kisses, they found time to discuss her immediate need for a secretarial job, and Harding had become somewhat "less inclined to recommend me in Washington." He would think of something else. Meanwhile, he tucked a thirty dollar bill in her new silk stocking, and then they parted.

On his next visit to New York, Harding took Nan with him to a speaking engagement. In the taxi as they drove, Harding asked how fast she thought she could take dictation. She thought she could not go too fast.

"Well, look here," said Harding, "I'll dictate a letter to you and you tell me whether you 'get' all of it."

Harding dictated: "My darling Nan: I love you more than the

In pearls and mink (or fox), Nan Britton of Marion seems worldlier and more glamorous, more the flapper and the vamp than she ever quite was. (United Press International Photo)

world, and I want you to belong to me. Could you belong to me, dearie? I want you . . . and I need you so. . . ."

Nan silenced him "with the kisses he pleaded for."

Harding took her at once to the Empire Building at 71 Broadway, to the office of the chairman of the board of the United States Steel Corporation, Judge Elbert H. Gary. Judge Gary introduced Nan to the comptroller of the company, saying: "Mr. Filbert, I want to help Senator Harding to help this young lady." She was hired.

On the way back down in the elevator, Harding whispered to Nan, "*Now,* do you believe that I love you?"

Back in the bridal chamber at the Manhattan Hotel, they cuddled together in a big armchair. "I love you, dearie," Harding said. "We were made for each other, Nan." Still, the bed remained undisturbed.

Her job was in Chicago—a safer place than either Washington or New York. They met several times more, when Harding's speaking engagements took him to the Middle West, and Nan coyly managed to slip away from his suggestions, and, finally, his direct question: "Dearie, 'r y' going t' sleep with me?"

On one train ride together, they shared a berth. "I had early reached this conclusion," Nan said: "People got married and undressed and slept together; therefore, one must be undressed in order for any harm to come to them. I remember that this belief was so strong in my mind that when, during our ride together from Connersville to Chicago, I experienced sweet thrills from just having Mr. Harding's hands upon the outside of my nightdress, I became panic-stricken. I inquired tearfully whether he really thought I would have a child right away. Of course this absurdity amused him greatly, but the fact that I was so ignorant seemed to add to his cherishment of me for some reason. And I loved him so dearly."

In July of 1917, Harding and Nan met once again in New York and repaired, this time, to a hotel on Broadway in the Thirties. "I remember so well I wore a pink linen dress which was rather short and enhanced the little-girl look which was often my despair. . . . There were no words going up in the elevator.

"The day was exceedingly warm and we were glad to see that the room which had been assigned to us had two large windows. The boy threw them open for us and left. The room faced Broadway, but we were high enough not to be bothered by street noises. We were quite alone."

They had shared a bed so often by this time, Nan was so truly fond of him, her resistance had become too tedious a burden for her to maintain, it was hot, and, somehow, the standards of brisker days dissolved.

"I became Mr. Harding's bride—as he called me—on that day." If it seemed anticlimatic—evoking no rapturous reminiscences on Nan's part—at least she was not dismayed. She had moved to a job in New York then, and Harding would come up from Washington at least once a week to spend the night with Nan in one shabby hotel or another, and Nan's passion did not fade. Often, when she wrote to him from the little table next to her bed in a room she rented in the apartment of an older couple, she would look up into an oval mirror above her writing table, "and smile at the girl who smiled back at me knowing, as I knew, that she was the sweetheart of the man who was to me easily the most desirable man in all the world. I studied the features of this girl in the mirror . . . minutely, to discover for myself just *why* he had chosen to love her! Sometimes . . . I would glance up and catch the soft lights in the eyes of the girl in the mirror which were the tell-tale lights of worshipping love or languishing passion."

Sometimes they would meet outside New York, if Harding had a speaking engagement somewhere else. He would write to Nan, enclosing money, and give her gentle but exact instructions about just which train to take, when and where to arrive, how to register.

"I shall never forget," she said of one such meeting, "how the sun was streaming in at the windows in the hotel when Mr. Harding opened the door in his pajamas in answer to my rather timid knock. His face was all smiles as he closed the door and took me in his arms. 'Gee, Nan, I'm s'glad t'see you!' he exclaimed. I just loved the way he lapsed into the vernacular when we were alone together. . . . We strolled out into the country. . . . He could have chosen no lovelier spot than the sunny meadow where we spent the morning. It sloped gently down to a winding stream, and on one side there was a thick wood. The ground was soft and the grass high. . . ."

Once they met in New Jersey, where Harding was to give a speech at the armory in Elizabeth. They were to meet before he spoke, but Nan was late; and, afterwards, he said, he had to get back to Washington. But, Nan asked, couldn't she then ride back down to Washington on the train with him? "Why, dearie, they're stopping a special train for me–a through train–and I couldn't explain having you with me. Now you take the first train back to New York and I'll be over soon, I promise you!"

"Which I did, of course," Nan recalled. "And he kept his promise."

Their times together were usually brief, but occasionally Harding would be able to spend the whole afternoon and evening with Nan–as he did one time in the Senate Office Building in Washington. Sometimes he would arrive in New York unexpectedly as he did once in midwinter, asking Nan if she could get the afternoon off. Nan told her boss that her sweetheart had arrived unexpectedly. Her boss knew, she said, "as everybody else in the office knew, of course, that I had a sweetheart who lived in Washington. I usually referred to him as 'my man.' "

She borrowed the apartment of a friend, and Harding arrived, getting off the elevator on the floor below, to allay any suspicions on the part of the elevator man, and they spent "a most intimate afternoon. How indelible," said Nan, "my memory of Mr. Harding sitting on the day bed, his back against the wall, holding me in his arms and looking down at me with a smile that was so sweet that it made me want to cry from sheer contentment! 'Happy, dearie?' he asked."

"How I *loved,*" Nan said, "to hear him say 'dearie'!"

They went to the theater often. One night they saw Al Jolson in *Sinbad, the Sailor* at the Winter Garden. Nan did not much like the show and betrayed her impatience by starting to put on her gloves and her wrap. " 'Where are you going, Nan?' Mr. Harding asked in gentle rebuke. If ever there was anyone thoughtful of others, it was Warren Harding, and it is likely that, being a speaker himself, he wished to extend all possible courtesy and attentiveness to others who held the stage."

From time to time they talked about how wonderful it would be to have a child, concluding, of course, that such a thing was strictly impossible. Harding had never had a child, and he told Nan that he had really wanted to adopt one, but Mrs. Harding would not hear of it. "I used to think," said Nan, "Mr. Harding might have liked to adopt *me,* though he never said so to me. However, he spoke very freely to me about what he would do if Mrs. Harding were to pass on–he wanted to buy a place for us and live in the country, and often during those days Mr. Harding said to me, 'Wouldn't that be grand, Nan? You'd make such a darling wife!' "

He gave her presents, of money or boxes of candy, and they would go out to after-theater suppers that were "so sweetly intimate and it was a joy just to sit and look at him." He would put especially choice morsels of food on her plate, caring for her as for a daughter, and occasionally she would catch his attention of a sudden, and he would say, "That's a very becoming hat, Nan," or "God, Nan, you're pretty!" And, when they were apart, he wrote her letters, wonderful letters, forty and sixty pages long.

Unlike Carrie, Nan did not resent Harding's preoccupation with getting ahead as a politician. On the contrary, she always told him that she thought he would one day be president. She loved more than anything to think what an important man he was, how powerful, how famous. She loved it especially when they would be leaving a restaurant, and she would hear one of the diners exclaim, "There goes Harding!"

XIV.

The Available Man

ANY AMERICAN BOY might grow up to be president of the United States, but when it comes time to choose a candidate to run for the office, some men seem to be more available than others. Any man over the age of thirty-five, who is not in jail, who has not been convicted, or recently convicted, of a crime, who has been married but not divorced, is, perhaps, somewhat more available for office than others. A man who has proven himself a loyal worker for one of the two major parties is certainly more available than others, however; and any Ohioan with these qualifications in Harding's day would have been even more available, since Ohio was the presidential state. Any Ohioan with these qualifications who held a major elective office, whose political adversaries back home had recently been defeated for reelection, who had taken pains to be cordial to all factions back home, would be among the most available men—and, in a time that the Democratic president of the

United States, Woodrow Wilson, was concluding a hopeless, pointless bloody, stupid war, any Republican politician with all these qualifications was so available as almost to have it.

The trick for a politician is to announce his availability, and Harding managed that by resorting to the old device of starting a rumor by denying it. "Honestly," he wrote to one of his old pals in the Ohio legislature, "I would not have [the presidency] if I could reach out and grasp it, and I really do not want any of my friends to promote it in any way. . . . I find it difficult to make a good many people believe that one can feel this way. . . . Of course, I am human enough to enjoy having friends who think well enough of me to suggest me for the position, and I confess some pleasure in knowing that events have so broken thus far that I should attract some favorable mention, but when it comes down to serious consideration I am wholly truthful when I say that I had rather no mention were made whatever."

If an available man has decided to take this passive approach to the presidency, rather than, as others have done, to grab at it, then he must sit back and wait for a booster to come along and promote his candidacy, and he must take (without seeming to want to) whatever booster he can get. Of all the promoters who came his way, the best that Harding could attract without encouragement was Harry Daugherty.

Daugherty, a grabber by temperament, thought Harding was a hopelessly dimwitted, backward fellow who had to be shaped into a presidential candidate against his will—and afterward, once Daugherty had got the presidential campaign underway, he took full credit for being a kingmaker. "I found him," Daugherty said of Harding, "sunning himself, like a turtle on a log, and I pushed him into the water."

The campaign that Daugherty thought he designed and forced on Harding was the classic Ohio strategy: to hang back, help maneuver the convention into a deadlock, and take the nomination as the natural compromise candidate from that great presidential state in the middle of America, Ohio.

The great obstacle to this strategy was Teddy Roosevelt, who was willing, for the sake of being elected president again, to scuttle the Progressives and become a loyal Republican once more. If Roosevelt wanted the nomination, no one was more available than he was, and Harding took pains to ingratiate himself with Roosevelt, writing complimentary letters to the old Rough Rider until Roosevelt finally invited Harding to a meeting to consider ways in which the old Republican party might be brought back together again. "We did not dwell on the differences of 1912," Harding said after the meeting, "for that was an old story."

In January of 1919, Teddy Roosevelt died. "I have some ideas," Daugherty wrote Harding on the day of the funeral, "about this thing now which I will talk over with you." Harding wrote an old friend in Ohio that "the death of Col. Roosevelt will somewhat change the plans of some Republicans of Ohio, especially in their attitude toward state organization. I may be over-confident about the situation, but I think we are going to be able to organize without any serious friction." That is to say, Harding now expected, with the Roosevelt faction in Ohio leaderless, to keep the Ohio organization solidly behind him as the favorite son candidate for 1920.

Harding delivered a eulogy to the Ohio state legislature: before Roosevelt died, said Harding, the great man had spoken from his heart, privately, to Harding. "Harding," he had said, "we have all got to get together and restore the Republican party to power in order to save this great country of ours." Roosevelt, Harding mused, had really been "less the radical than he ofttimes appeared." He had been, really, it might be said, more a champion of party harmony and loyalty.

Daugherty, meanwhile, took to the road and called on the political bosses of key states. Daugherty did not ask any of the bosses to support Harding outright. Harding did not wish to stand out against the wishes of any of the party leaders. Harding wanted the leaders to do whatever they wished. Daugherty asked only this: if a fellow's first choice seemed unable to get the nomination, then

Harding would merely like to be second choice. He would like to be everyone's second choice.

"Truly, my dear Reily," Harding wrote to an old friend, "I do not wish my friends to make any effort to make me a candidate. . . . I know better than some who over-estimate both my ability and my availability. . . . I do not wish to be considered in connection with the nomination for our Party."

"I expect," he wrote, tirelessly, to another old friend, "it is very possible that I would make as good a President as a great many men who are talked of for that position. . . . At the same time I have such a sure understanding of my own inefficiency that I should really be ashamed to presume myself fitted to reach out for a place of such responsibility. More than that, I would not think of involving my many good friends in the tremendous tasks of making a Presidential campaign."

To another friend, he wrote, "I cannot for the life of me see why anybody would deliberately shoulder the annoyance and worries and incessant trials incident to a campaign for nomination and election to . . ."

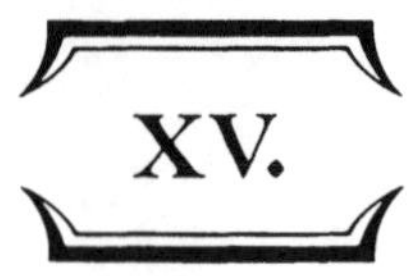

XV.

A Blessed, Though Quiet, Event

IT WAS TOWARD the end of February 1919, that Nan became certain beyond any doubt "that I was to become the mother of Warren Harding's child. . . . I wrote Mr. Harding as soon as my belief was confirmed in my own mind.

"The effect of Mr. Harding's letters whenever I was perturbed over anything was to calm me, and he wrote that this trouble was not so very serious and could be handled."

Nan arrived in Washington and went to the Hotel Willard, where Harding joined her in her room. "I remember well, how, in spite of the fact that his forehead was wet and he showed other signs of nervousness, he said in the low voice which always soothed me, 'We must go at this thing in a sane way, dearie, and we must not allow ourselves to be nervous over it.' "

The way he suggested handling the situation was to give Nan a small bottle of Dr. Humphrey's No. 11 tablets. Nan was suspicious of the medicine; she had not thought of inducing an abortion so much as of having Harding's child. He took her onto his lap and talked, as he often had before, of the day when he would be finished with politics, of getting a farm with dogs and horses, chickens and pigs, and, of course, a bride.

"As he talked his voice grew tense. His hands trembled visibly. I took one of them in mine and held it tightly. . . . I had never seen him so moved, so shaken . . . 'and I would take you out there, Nan darling, as–my–wife. . . .' He freed his hand with sudden force and grasped both my arms tightly. 'Look at me, dearie!' he cried, 'you *would* be my wife, wouldn't you? You would marry me, Nan? Oh, dearie, dearie,' brokenly, 'if I only could . . . if we only could have our child–together!' This last came as a hushed exclamation, almost a prayer, scarcely audible. The yearning of a heart laid bare! I nodded wordlessly. The air seemed sacred.

"When he spoke again it was as if he had returned to stern realities. . . . He smiled at me sadly. 'Would be grand, wouldn't it, dearie?' . . . He repeated it and looked out the window at his left. The voice grew stern again; he did not smile now; only just turned and looked at me hard as a man might who is trying not to cry. . . ."

Nonetheless, Nan went ahead and had their child, a daughter. Near the end of her pregnancy, Nan repaired to the Hotel Monmouth in Asbury Park, New Jersey, just a block from the ocean–and then, feeling awkward at the hotel, to a private rooming house nearby. The child was born on the afternoon of October 22, and Nan could not have been more pleased.

When her daughter was six weeks old, Nan went into New York to do some Christmas shopping, and to phone Harding–something she felt she could not do from her rooming house in Asbury Park. She felt weak and inexpressibly sad, and when she got Harding on the phone, he said no more than "Hello," and she began to cry. She asked him when he felt she might be strong again; she felt so weak; and he urged her to return to Asbury Park to rest. She wished she could see him, that he might come to New

York just for a short visit, but he said he could not. "He said he was in fact coming over to New York, but he thought it unwise for us to be seen together. . . ." Nor did Harding ever find it prudent to see his only child.

The Smoke-Filled Room

"I DON'T EXPECT Senator Harding to be nominated on the first, second, or third ballot," Harry Daugherty said, shooting his mouth off to some newspaper reporters a few months before the convention, "but I think about eleven minutes after two o'clock on Friday morning of the convention, when fifteen or twenty men, bleary-eyed and perspiring profusely from the heat, are sitting around a table, some one of them will say: 'Who will we nominate?' At the decisive time the friends of Senator Harding can suggest him and can afford to abide by the result. I don't know but what I might suggest him myself." When the newspapermen wrote up their interview with Daugherty, one of them added that the politicians would be sitting around a table smoking cigars, and so the legend of the "smoke-filled room" entered the lexicon of American politics.

The front-runner for the Republican nomination in 1920 was General Leonard Wood, a ramrod New Englander who sported a riding crop and declared himself in favor of a strong central government and opposed to the Communist menace. He would have made an acceptable Republican candidate except that he had a taint of Progressivism about him—having been a friend of Teddy Roosevelt. Although the war against the Progressives was officially ended, and Teddy Roosevelt was back in the pantheon of party heroes, nonetheless, the bosses were not eager to embrace a Progressive. When Wood's campaign manager began to make some deals with the bosses to line up their support, they started to soften somewhat; but then Wood, in a fit of high-mindedness, fired his campaign manager for making shady deals. The Old Guard concluded immediately that Wood was not a reasonable man, and they began to look around for another candidate, any other candidate, that they could use to stop Wood.

Herbert Hoover was available. He had a good record as administrator of European relief during World War I; indeed, his name had become a popular verb: to Hooverize meant to save food. The trouble with Hoover was that no one knew whether he was a Republican or a Democrat, and the bosses were not inclined to take any more risks.

Senator Hiram Johnson of California was available. He was a good orator and an agreeable man. Unfortunately, he insisted on campaigning in a Rough Rider hat and displaying photographs of Teddy Roosevelt in his campaign headquarters. He could hardly be considered altogether reasonable.

Frank O. Lowden, the governor of Illinois, had the greatest popular appeal after Wood and Hoover. Unhappily, as governor he had established a record as a reformer, and it was not entirely clear that he was a reasonable candidate. He seemed, however, to want to talk with the bosses, and so the bosses decided to ease their support behind Lowden—at least for long enough to stop Wood.

The job of party bosses is not, as is commonly supposed, to choose a presidential candidate for office. The job of party bosses is to eliminate unacceptable candidates from the field and then permit a free choice among the remaining field of reasonable men.

All of the most popular candidates, it seemed, were Progressives in one fashion or another. Evidently most Americans were eager for some sort of reform candidate–which made the task of the bosses more difficult. The primaries helped. As the gaggle of reformers went into the primaries, they bumped up against one another, split the votes, and made one another appear to be "weak" candidates. Wood came out of the primaries with the most votes; he had 124 committed delegates to 112 for Johnson and 72 for Lowden. But Wood's victory had not been strong enough. The bosses moved with renewed conviction behind Lowden.

It was then that Harry Daugherty earned his position as campaign manager. General Wood's campaign manager had raised a lot of money for his candidate and spent too lavishly. He had done nothing wrong, nothing illegal–but he had taken too much money from rich easterners. Daugherty found out who had contributed money to Wood, and slipped the names of these fat cats to Senator Borah, one of Hiram Johnson's supporters.

In the Senate, Senator Borah gave a blistering speech against Wood's attempt to "buy" the presidency. Borah called for a special committee to inquire into the matter of Wood's campaign expenditures.

The Senate committee found that Wood had spent almost two million dollars that could be accounted for–and probably another six million that could not be accounted for. Although they found nothing illegal, the sum of money was shocking. Wood seemed less and less a "popular" candidate, more and more a candidate of the bankers of the East.

The Senate committee, in order to be evenhanded, reported on the finances of the other candidates, too. Lowden, they discovered, had only spent $400,000 that they could account for, but some of this money had clearly been spent in the South for the outright buying of delegate votes at the rate of $2,500 apiece. Lowden's candidacy was severely damaged.

But Johnson's candidacy was ruined, too. Nothing was found to be wrong with his finances; but, because it was his friend Borah who had started all the trouble, the bosses were even more determined to deny him the nomination.

By the time the delegates gathered in Chicago in June, no one much liked any one of the candidates, although the delegates remained committed to the leading contenders because they could find no one else they liked either.

Still, the old regulars were resourceful. They could, if nothing else, give the appearance of being completely in control of the convention so that the delegates, thinking the bosses were in control, would follow orders; and the bosses, by seeming to boss the convention, would boss it. They chose Senator Henry Cabot Lodge, the little goateed autocrat of Massachusetts, who could not even get his home state to nominate him as a favorite son candidate for president, to be the permanent chairman of the convention–and Lodge moved the delegates swiftly through the preliminaries and formalities into the balloting–where the bosses hoped to arrange a real, or apparent, deadlock.

On the first ballot, General Wood unnerved the bosses by getting fully 287½ votes, fifty more than had been anticipated. Lowden was second with 211; and Johnson was third with 133½. (Harding, with his Ohio ballots and a few other votes, appeared with 65½ votes down among a welter of favorite sons, including Nicholas Murray Butler of New York, William Sproul of Pennsylvania, Coolidge, and even La Follette.)

On the second ballot, some of the votes that were being held back by party leaders were brought neatly in behind Lowden to make it seem that a trend was developing against Wood. Even Daugherty let a couple of votes go to Lowden, allowing Harding's count to drop to 59. Butler released 10 delegates, and some of the organization southerners moved in behind Lowden.

Without a moment's hesitation, Lodge took the delegates into the third ballot, and the bosses moved more votes over to Lowden, 16 of them from Butler, for a total of 23 new votes for the

Frank Brandegee, the portly, tough-talking Senator from Connecticut, explained Harding's candidacy for the presidency: "There ain't any first-raters this year."

Illinois governor. But, at that point the reserves of the bosses had almost run out, and no one was following the unconvincing "trend." Instead, Wood was gaining handsomely, and on the fourth ballot, Wood got 314½ votes, only 177 short of the total needed for nomination. The Old Guard was able to muster only another 6½ votes for Lowden. The offensive was slipping; soon it would falter, and its weakness would be apparent to all the convention delegates. Wood's momentum needed to be stopped.

"I move," said Senator Smoot, "that the convention do adjourn until tomorrow morning at ten o'clock."

"Those in favor," Lodge said immediately, ". . . will signify by saying 'Aye.' "

There was a scattering of "Ayes."

"Those opposed, 'No.' "

The coliseum trembled with a booming chorus of "NO!"

"The ayes have it," Lodge said in a voice of profound boredom, put down his gavel, and walked off the platform.

"There's going to be a deadlock," Smoot said to the reporters who gathered in bewilderment around him, "and we'll have to work out some solution; we wanted the night to think it over."

In the Blackstone Hotel, Will Hays, chairman of the national committee, shared a suite of rooms on the thirteenth floor with George Harvey, a solemn man who took himself very seriously, the editor of the *North American Review,* intimate of J. P. Morgan partners. That night, politicians of all sorts drifted through the

Henry Cabot Lodge—dapper, stiff-necked, and dreadfully proud—was well-known to the voters back in his home state of Massachusetts: they would not even deign to send him to the convention as their favorite son candidate for president. The bosses thought much better of him and appointed him chairman of the convention.

rooms of Harvey and Hays, mostly to confer with Hays. Having declared a deadlock, the bosses now labored to resolve it. Many names were mentioned. Harvey thought that Will Hays himself would make a fine candidate. Someone suggested Charles Evans Hughes of New York. No one seemed to be anyone's clear first choice.

Senator Knox of Pennsylvania, said Samuel Hopkins Adams, "had a bad heart. . . . Governor Sproul was too local. Senator Jim Watson was too hidebound a standpatter. . . . Geographical considerations worked against Coolidge; he was too far east. Hoover? What was Hoover?"

"It was," Senator Wadsworth said, "a sort of continuous performance. I was in and out of the room several times that night. They were like a lot of chickens with their heads off. They had no program and no definite affirmative decision was reached." It was a smoke-filled room, very close to just the sort of thing that Daugherty had in mind, but Daugherty himself was not there, and the bosses were less in control of things than people usually imagine.

In the course of the night, Watson of Indiana dropped by, McCormick of Illinois, Weeks of Massachusetts, and dozens of others. Senator Lodge stayed–sitting composedly, swinging one leg, boosting no one, embracing no cause or candidate, but summarizing the points for and against each candidate as his name was mentioned, shaking his head over one name, pointing out the unreliability of another. As one after another of the possibilities was eliminated, only one candidate remained available, the one against whom no one had a particular objection, everyone's second choice, Warren Harding.

Those who were still in the room at about two o'clock in the morning–Lodge, McCormick, Calder of New York, Curtis of Kansas, Smoot of Utah, Brandegee of Connecticut, Watson of Indiana, and Hays and Harvey thought they might give Harding a run for it the next day. If Harding could not make it in four or five ballots, then they would have to turn to another.

Harvey called Harding to the suite. Harding, exhausted, rumpled, lacking a good shave, and having despaired of getting the nomination, was taken aside. "We think," said Harvey, "you may be nominated tomorrow; before acting finally, we think you should tell us, on your conscience and before God, whether there is anything that might be brought up against you that would embarrass the party, any impediment that might disqualify you or make you inexpedient, either as candidate or as President."

Harding, stunned, asked to have a few moments to think it over, and Harvey left him alone in one of the rooms of the suite. Had it ever been true that he did not want the nomination, this was his chance to avoid it. Ten minutes later, Harding emerged from the room. He had thought it over. No, on his conscience and before God, he could think of nothing.

Harvey quickly called in a couple of reporters and let them have an interview with Brandegee and some of the other senators. The leaders explained to the reporters that, since Lowden and Wood were deadlocked, they had decided that Harding was the "logical" choice of the convention. He could be trusted to "go along" with Congress, he looked like a president. One of the reporters was astonished: Harding was barely known outside Ohio. Brandegee said he would be known after he was nominated. "There ain't any first-raters this year. This ain't 1880 or any 1904; we haven't any John Shermans or Theodore Roosevelts; we got a lot of second-raters and Warren Harding is the best of the second-raters."

Senator Smoot was quick to grant an interview to a reporter from the New York *Telegram* out in the corridor. Harding was the man, said Smoot: the bosses would put him over the next afternoon after giving Lowden a brief run.

A Harvard graduate and an alcoholic, Boise Penrose, the disheveled boss of Pennsylvania, was too indisposed to attend the convention, and so—as a boss of the bosses—he phoned in his orders, swinging his support, finally, to Harding.

The point was to seem to be in charge, to announce at once that the fix was in, to tell the reporters and spread the word, to make it seem a *fait accompli* because the moment was, in fact, extremely perilous. Other meetings were going on that night. Wood and Lowden might decide to join forces and take the nomination as president and vice-president. Or one of them might join with Hiram Johnson. They were all meeting with one another.

The bosses would have to sustain the deadlock the next day,

make certain that it did not slip, and then gradually, carefully, move a few delegates at a time behind Harding to make a trend.

At ten o'clock the next morning, Lodge called for the fifth ballot. Wood lost 15½ votes at once, slipping to 299, and Lowden jumped ahead to 303. Johnson slipped a few votes, and Harding picked up a few to get a total of 78. The move had begun slowly, with apparently complete control: no surprises, no sudden shifts.

On the sixth ballot, Wood's managers called out every last vote they could get. Lowden and Wood tied at 311½. Johnson slipped another 23½ votes to 114. The rumor had begun to spread on the floor that Harding was the choice of the bosses, that he would be put over after a few more ballots, nothing could stop him, and the delegates had better jump on the bandwagon. Harding got 89 votes.

On the seventh ballot, Wood and Lowden continued to hold each other. Wood got 312, Lowden 311½. Johnson slipped precipitously to 90½. Harding moved smartly up to 105. The trend was developing.

The eighth ballot began at about one o'clock in the afternoon. The temperature in the coliseum was about 100. The delegates were in despair, moving around looking for air, fanning themselves. They were ready to make a decision. Wood lost 22 votes, going down to 290. The nearly implacable law of convention voting is that a leader must remain a leader. A loss of 22 votes is a countertrend. Wood's candidacy was over. Lowden slipped down to 307. His candidacy was not demolished, but the loss of a few votes was frightening. Johnson's delegates were deserting him steadily. Harding came through with a booming 133½ votes.

Daugherty thought that the next ballot would establish the break to Harding. He sent all his men around the hall to bring in the votes that had been held back or placed elsewhere, hidden behind favorite sons or kept behind Lowden or Wood. In truth, Harding was attracting individual votes here and there around the hall–not large blocs of bossed votes, but individual votes of delegates who believed that the bosses were controlling things. Harding

General Leonard Wood—ramrod honest, forthright, popular, the preferred candidate of the people—was finally stopped by the bosses on the eighth ballot.

was winning, but he was not winning because the bosses had begun to move the votes over to him. He was winning—although none of the delegates knew it, and Harding himself did not know it, and would not have believed it—on his own.

One of Lowden's men called for a recess. The moment had come, now that Harding's nomination was assured, for some last-minute deals. Lodge called for a vote. Once more there were a few scattered votes in favor of recess, and a great chorus of noes against recess. Once again Lodge declared that the ayes had it and adjourned the convention for a few hours.

It was said that a deal would be made to give Hiram Johnson the vice-presidency, in order to placate the Progressives. It was said that Wood and Lowden were finally going to join forces to go on the ticket as President and Vice President. It was said that Lowden was making some sort of deal with Harding. In fact, nothing happened, except that Harding and Lowden, the two candidates who

Senator Lodge, the autocrat of the speaker's platform, presides over the unruly, perspiring delegates with firm gentility.

had both had, in different ways, the favor of the bosses, met and shook hands, and Lowden gave the word to release his delegates to Harding. Lowden had proved himself a loyal party man. He would be offered many consolations.

The first indication of what had happened during the recess came when the convention was called back to order, and the roll call for the ninth ballot reached Connecticut–Senator Brandegee's state, which had been giving 13 votes to Lowden on the preceding ballots. All 13 votes went to Harding. Then, when Kansas was called, the big break occurred: 20 votes for Harding. "The Coliseum was in an uproar," Daugherty recalled. "Police were hurled aside like children. Smoot and Lodge hammered their gavels in vain. When Ohio was called a hush fell over the sweltering mass. Every man except our delegates expected, of course, a solid vote at last from Harding's own state. And when . . . nine men still voted for Wood the most extraordinary thing happened that I ever witnessed in a national convention. Their vote was greeted with a sullen roar of indignation and surprise. Hoots, cat-calls, boos, yells, and hisses swept through the delegates." Still, by the end of the ballot, Harding led the pack with 374 votes. Wood had 249. Lowden, who had let most of his delegates move to Harding, still kept 121½.

"Our men," said Daugherty, "leaped to their feet and yelled themselves hoarse. They marched down the aisles with banners and streamers, and exhorted sinners to repent before it was too late.

" 'Come on, boys!'

" 'It's all over!'

" 'Climb on the bandwagon!' "

Daugherty looked up into the boxes and caught sight of Mrs. Harding. He suddenly thought that Mrs. Harding might be so amazed by what was about to happen on the next ballot that she would have a heart attack. He rushed upstairs to join her.

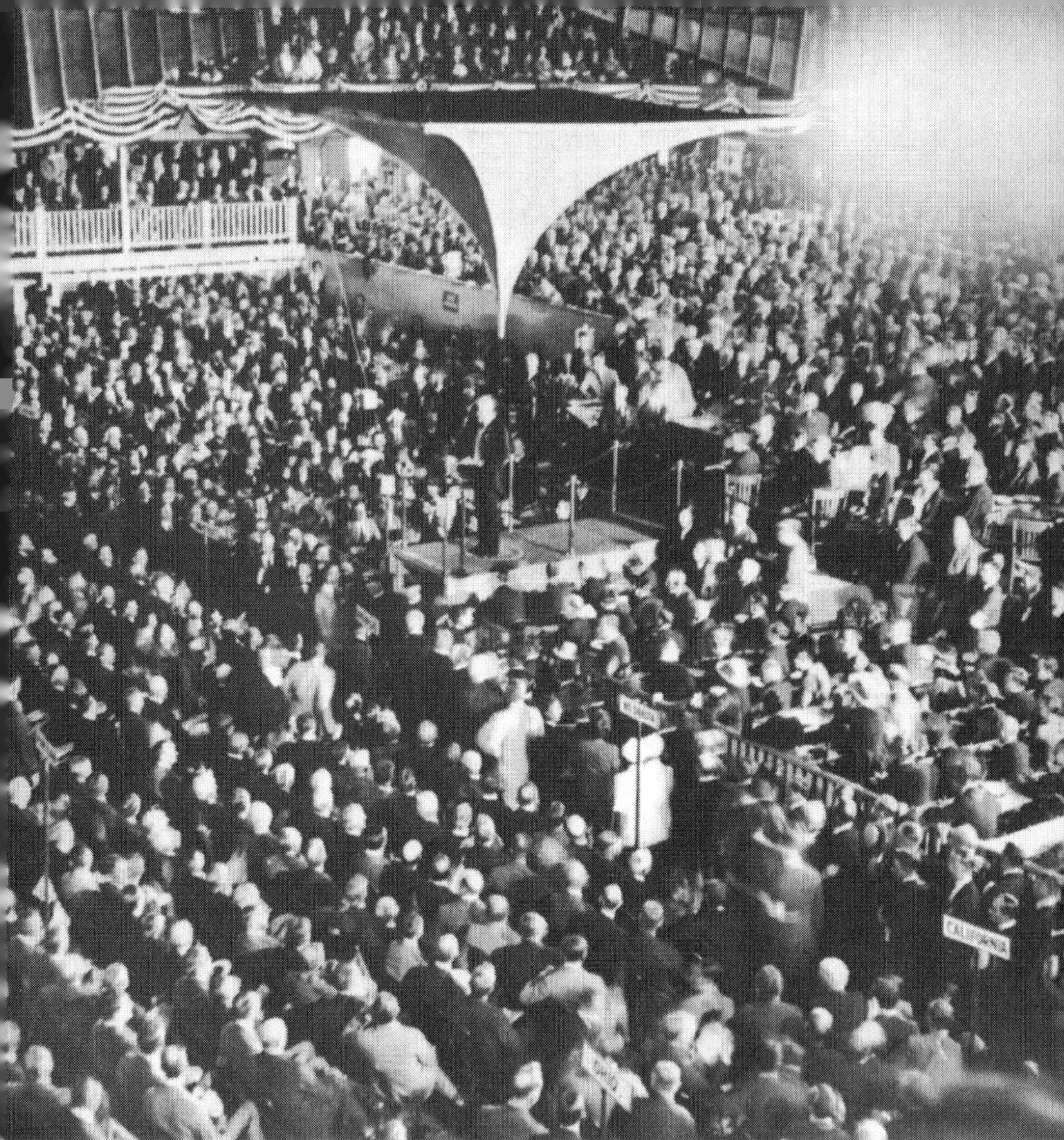

"She had removed her hat in the sweltering heat and sat humped forward in her chair, her arms tightly folded. In her right hand she gripped two enormous hatpins, in vogue at the time. I drew a chair close beside her and she started at the touch of my hand on her arm. A deep frown shadowed her face.

"'It's terrible, isn't it?'

"'What?'

"'All this wild excitement. . . . I can't follow it–'

" 'I didn't think you would, but something's going to happen down there in a few minutes that may shock you if you don't look out–'

" 'What do you mean?' she asked sharply.

". . . I leaned closer and whispered: 'We have the votes. Your husband will be nominated on the next ballot–'

"She gave a sudden start, fairly leaped from her chair. The movement drove both hatpins deep into my side.

"I sprang back and felt the blood follow them. . . . I had come to save a woman's life and she had unwittingly murdered me! I said nothing to disturb her but felt my head swimming as the blood began to run down my leg and fill my shoe. For a moment I swayed, about to faint. I was smothering. . . . I felt my way down to the floor of the Convention and listened to the roll call with a vague sense of detachment. . . . When I walked I could hear the queer swish of the blood that filled my shoe. I felt my body sway, and caught a chair. I was smothering again."

By the time the clerk had got to Pennsylvania, Harding had 440 votes. He needed 53 more for the nomination. "Pennsylvania," the head of the delegation called out in a deep voice, "casts sixty-one votes for Warren G. Harding!"

"A cheer rose that shook the earth," Daugherty said. "The vast spaces of the Coliseum echoed with demoniac screams. Ambitions crumbled! . . . I tottered to my room, and examined myself. My lung had not been pierced. My smothering was only in imagination. My shoe was full of perspiration."

Frelinghuysen of New Jersey moved to make the nomination unanimous. Lodge called for the ayes, and this time the vote was thunderously in favor of the motion. Lodge called for the noes. There were some emphatic bellows of no from the floor. Lodge ruled the vote unanimous.

Nan Britton watched from a seat high up in the gallery. "How could that surging multitude–cheering and whistling and stampeding the aisles with their Harding banners held aloft–be interested anyway in the tumult of unutterable emotion that rose within me? My eyes swam. . . ."

It was said that he was the candidate of the bosses–and that was true, but it was only part of the truth. In fact, he had won the nomination because he knew how to be a reasonable man, a sound man, a man who was able to blend in, a loyal man, a man who knew how to be conciliatory, to forgive a slight, to bear no grudge, to despise no man's eccentricities or weaknesses, a man who knew how to wait and when to move, a man who knew how to carry himself and dress and smile like a president of the United States–all of these qualities and talents had combined to make him the most available man in America. And he had acquired them all by himself.

"I feel," said the new Republican nominee for president, "like a man who goes in on a pair of eights and comes out with aces full."

XVII.

Carrie Takes Another Vacation

SOME OF THE hard-eyed members of the Republican Old Guard found out about Carrie Phillips soon enough, and Harding was told that something would need to be done about her. Harding and Carrie had not been in touch for several years. Perhaps it is some measure of the love they once felt for one another that they came now to a moment of such fierce coldness. One of Harding's men was dispatched to talk to Carrie. He offered her an outright bribe of $20,000 plus an additional monthly stipend, to be paid for as long as Harding was in office, plus an all-expense-paid trip around the world for Carrie and her husband, providing they both took the trip right away and stayed out of the country until the election was over. It is some measure of her feelings for her former lover that she took the deal without a moment's hesitation.

The Front Porch Campaign

HARDING CHOSE, CANNILY, to stay on his own front porch to campaign for the presidency. The front yard was covered with crushed gravel to make certain that the crowds would not churn it into mud, and the procession began of brass bands and marching clubs, the Elks, the Moose, the Knights of Pythias, the Ohio State Dental Association, small children, neighbors, actors and actresses, the all but forgotten candidate for vice-president, Calvin Coolidge of Vermont, veterinary organizations, Chief Red Fox, the alumni of Iberia College. And the picture was spread across America of a man of calm and dignity, not a man who shouted and harangued out on the hustings, but a man who loved to stay at home, enjoyed seeing the little children drop by his house, a family man, decent and dependable, a man who liked to pitch horseshoes and pat little children on the head, a man who stood for the essential goodness of America, a man whose own equanimity would restore America to

Speaking from his own front porch, the candidate stands boldly in favor of America, children, fiscal responsibility, dogs, home towns, and, above all, normalcy.

balance and harmony, to the old values of neighborliness and love of country, cooperation and hard work, decorum and discretion, peace and security.

The country to which Harding addressed himself was still suffering from having fought the war to end war and having discovered that the lives lost in the war and the slogans and songs that had cheered the soldiers to their deaths had all been pointless. The country suffered not simply from the economic dislocations caused by the war–inflation, business failures, mortgage foreclosures, unemployment, reductions in wages–but also from bruised feelings, bitterness, and rage. The Ku Klux Klan and the American Legion and the I.W.W. all nourished and reacted to these passions. Reds were arrested; pacifists were convicted of sedition under the Espionage Act; and a jury acquitted, after two minutes' deliberation, a man named Frank Petroni, who had shot and killed Frank Petrich, an alien, for shouting, "To hell with the United States."

Sixteen packages in the New York General Post Office were found to contain dynamite; thirty-four mail bombs were discovered on their way through the postal service to public officials; four

On the campaign trail, Florence and Warren Harding both seem somewhat less certain than the entourage that accompanies them.

hundred soldiers invaded the offices of a Socialist newspaper and beat up some of the editors; Sacco and Vanzetti, Italian-American workingmen and radical leftists, were arrested for robbing and killing the paymaster and guard at their shoe factory; and race riots broke out between whites and blacks in the streets of Washington, D.C.

Harding promised a "return to normalcy," a phrase that meant many things to many people, but meant, to all of them—unlike, say, a "return to abnormalcy"—something good. It meant, on the whole, in addition to setting aside the bloodshed of war and mollifying the general unrest and discontent, a restoration of a golden age before the war, an age of tranquillity and prosperity when everyone fundamentally agreed upon what mattered and how to go about getting it, when everyone agreed that the rules of

The candidate juggles the three obligatory attributes of the politician: cigar, golf club, and small, protesting child. (Ohio Historical Society)

Calvin Coolidge, nominated for vice president as an afterthought, was soon forgotten.

Sporting a straw boater and a bow tie, Harding casts his ballot confidently.

society were basically fair and decent within a classless structure in a polity that was free–in short, a return to an age that never was.

Having long since discovered how to promote himself by promoting others, Harding was able to show every individual how to put himself first. It had been said of President Wilson that he thought too much of his abstract ideals, his League of Nations, his aspirations to be a great figure on the European continent.

On their way to the inauguration, the president-elect and Mrs. Harding bid a simple farewell to their Marion neighbors. (Ohio Historical Society)

"We do not mean to hold aloof," candidate Harding declared to a meeting of the Ohio Society, "we choose no isolation, we shun no duty. I like to rejoice in an American conscience, and in a big conception of our obligations to liberty, justice and civilization. . . ."

Nonetheless: "It is fine to idealize, but it is very practical to make sure our own house is in perfect order before we attempt the miracle of the Old-World stabilization.

"Call it the selfishness of nationality if you will, I think it an inspiration to patriotic devotion–

"To safeguard America first.

"To stabilize America first.

"To prosper America first.

"To think of America first.

"To exalt America first.

"To live for and revere America first."

Harding was elected president by the largest plurality ever given to a presidential candidate. "It wasn't a landslide," one of the professional politicians said, "it was an earthquake."

XIX.

The Hardings in the White House

"NO RUMOR COULD have exceeded the reality," Alice Roosevelt Longworth said, having tagged along with Congressman Longworth to a poker game in the White House. "The study was filled with cronies, Daugherty, Jess Smith . . . and others, the air heavy with tobacco smoke, trays with bottles containing every imaginable brand of whisky stood about, cards and poker chips ready at hand—a general atmosphere of waistcoat unbuttoned, feet on the desk, and spittoons alongside."

Harding thought he would like wienerwurst and sauerkraut for dinner, but Mrs. Harding thought they were unsuitable for the White House. Harding wanted toothpicks on the table, but Mrs. Harding thought they were vulgar. Harding wanted to chew tobacco, but Mrs. Harding would not allow it. "She says," Harding told a visitor, as he surreptitiously tucked a cut into his cheek, "cigars are all right, but it's undignified to chew."

Mrs. Harding was extremely nervous. Each time she and Evalyn Walsh McLean had been together at a reception with a group of the smart set, Mrs. Harding would ask Evalyn afterward, "What did they say about me?"

When William Allen White, the editor of the Emporia, Kansas, *Gazette* called at the White House, he found Mrs. Harding "well-groomed, neatly dressed and highly marcelled when in public. She had a determined mouth, but her eyes lacked decision. They reflected ambition, but they had a clouded, puzzled look, rather than the clear brightness which is associated with an active and logical mentality."

Samuel Hopkins Adams, one of the other journalists who kept a particularly close watch on the White House, thought Mrs. Harding "overdid it; she tried too hard to be a great lady. Uncertain of herself, she took refuge in volubility and effusiveness. . . . She was prone to be overrouged and overcoiffured, often overdressed."

As for Harding himself, when he first took office, he did not quite fit in at the White House. Several people noticed that his trousers were too long. In time, however, Mrs. Harding got him spruced up, so that one day when William Allen White came to call he noticed that the president was dressed "with exact sartorial propriety, with exactly the kind of boutonniere he should wear, with precisely the gray stripe in his trousers that the hour required, with a proper dark four-in-hand tied most carefully. For a moment or two, while he was offering cigars and moving festively out of the preliminaries of a formal conversation, he was socially and spiritually erect. But as we sat in the south sunshine flooding through the windows of his office, he warmed and melted and slouched a little."

He played golf at least twice a week, and he was overjoyed whenever he managed to shoot in the nineties. Colonel Starling of the Secret Service followed Harding around the course and kept

track of his score and of the side bets he kept making with those who played with him. "He played," Starling said, "as if his life depended on every shot, and he made so many bets that sometimes he was betting against himself."

He played most often at the Chevy Chase Club, and he loved to bet with his partner six dollars Nassau against their opponents: a bet of six dollars out, six dollars in, and six dollars across. He would lay a side bet with his partner on low score, and then, as the game moved along, he would double up his bets, betting on individual holes, and then on individual shots as they went down the fairway. "I had to keep accounts," said Starling, "and it was a job for a Philadelphia lawyer."

At the end of the round, the players would repair to a house set aside for the president at Chevy Chase. Starling would get out the key to the liquor cabinet and bring out the scotch and Bourbon, and a black man named Taylor would serve highballs while Starling made his calculations and announced the winners. Harding would take a single drink, and then, when the bets were settled, he would turn to Starling and say, "Telephone the Duchess and say I am on my way home."

President and Mrs. Harding, in the first flush of a new president's honeymoon in Washington, step out the front door of the White House. (Ohio Historical Society)

Twice a week, he would convene the poker sessions at the White House. Ohio friends, cabinet members, senators, visiting businessmen, and political acquaintances would gather after dinner. Never more than eight would sit at the table at one time, though the cast of characters would shift sometimes in the course of the evening. Mrs. Harding hovered, not playing, but fetching drinks—nervous, some thought, about letting Warren out of her sight. Daugherty called her "Ma"; Ned McLean called her "Boss"; and some of the other regulars picked up Harding's habit of calling her "Duchess."

"We played at a rectangular table in the north end of the room," said one of the regulars about the sessions in the White House library. At one session, he recalled, "the President sat at one

Evalyn Walsh McLean—gorgeous, bejeweled, feathered, and corsaged—remained Mrs. Harding's steadfast capital friend.

The president, properly attired in his cap and plus fours, loved to play golf and to bet on it, going out and coming in, hole by hole, and overall. Here he tees off at a course in Maine. (Ohio Historical Society)

end and Will Hays, who was then Postmaster General, at the other. The others were Albert Lasker, at the time chairman of the Shipping Board; Harry Daugherty, Ned McLean, Mrs. McLean, and Mrs. Harding. . . . I remember that it was very hot and that Albert Lasker took his coat off, displaying red suspenders two inches wide."

Nan visited the White House for the first time several months

To the sly pleasure of his friend, the president pretends to fish while wearing a business suit—and he seems to have hooked an old boot.

after the inauguration, in June—apparently at her own initiative. She made the arrangement through her Secret Service contact, Tim Slade, and he met her at her hotel in Washington when she arrived and took her to the White House.

"We entered the executive offices through the main office entrance, which is the entrance on the right of the White House portico, and passed through the hall leading to the Cabinet Room. . . ." There they waited for Harding—"Mr. Harding," as Nan still called him.

She was impressed by the long table in the Cabinet Room, "around which stood the substantial chairs of the . . . men who met there. . . . A fireplace, a clock on the mantelpiece, and a few pictures completed the furnishings. Mr. Harding's chair at the head of the table interested me most, and I stroked the back of it and sipped

stale water from a partially filled glass which stood on the table in front of the President's chair. So this was where sat the leaders of the greatest nation in the world!"

They had been waiting only a few minutes before Harding opened the door just behind his Cabinet Room chair. He greeted Nan cordially and instructed Slade to remain there in the Cabinet Room. He took Nan into the adjoining room, a small room with a single window, an anteroom, and then through another door into his private office. As soon as they were in his office, with the door

James (Long Jim) Barnes, winner of the American Open, looks on as Harding gets to hand the trophy for the British Open to the legendary, falsely modest Jock Hutchison.

closed behind them, he turned and took her in his arms "and told me what I could see in his face–that he was delighted to see me."

She looked carefully around his office, to fix it in her memory. His desk was large and seemed to have many drawers. Opposite the desk was a large fireplace, where, "Mr. Harding told me, he burned all the letters I sent him after he had committed their messages to his heart." On top of his desk was a portrait of his mother, and Nan noticed that fresh flowers stood on the desk just next to the picture.

Along one side of the room were windows that opened out onto the White House grounds, the green lawn–and, not far off, the president's guard. "Mr. Harding said to me that people seemed to have eyes in the sides of their heads down there and so we must be very circumspect. Whereupon he introduced me to the one place where, he said, he thought we *might* share kisses in safety. This was a small closet in the anteroom, evidently a place for hats and coats, but entirely empty most of the times we used it, for we repaired there many times in the course of my visits to the White House, and in the darkness of a space not more than five feet square the President of the United States and his adoring sweetheart made love."

The work of being president, however, was beyond Harding. "I can't make a damn thing out of this tax problem," he said to William Allen White one day. "I listen to one side and they seem right, and then–God!–I talk to the other side and they seem just as right, and here I am where I started. I know somewhere there is a book that will give me the truth, but hell! I couldn't read the book."

When Arthur Draper, the foreign correspondent for the New York *Tribune,* dropped by after a trip to Europe, Harding called in

In a bunting-draped box at the races, Harding could not be mistaken for a man who bet on all the right horses.

his political secretary Jud Welliver and said to Draper: "I don't know anything about this European stuff. You and Jud get together and he can tell me later; he handles these matters for me."

He had said, when he had been a senator, that he thought he was not fitted to be president–and, of course, it had seemed that he was hoping to be contradicted. But the expressions of unease came more frequently now, until they became a common theme of his conversation. "Judge," he said to one of his companions after a round of golf, "I don't think I'm big enough for the Presidency." And, to a newspaper columnist he said, as they talked in his office, "Oftentimes, as I sit here, I don't seem to grasp that I am President."

According to the chief usher of the White House, Ike Hoover, Harding read no books, attended few plays, listened to no music–and seemed always to be plagued with anxieties. Hoover had served ten presidents, and he said Harding worked harder and slept less than any of the others. He seemed to want to do a good job. He paced the corridors of the White House restlessly, day and night.

Pillars of Society

TWICE A WEEK, every Tuesday and Friday morning, the members of the cabinet gathered around the polished table in the big room with the highbacked leather chairs next to Harding's office. Daugherty was there, of course, as attorney general, appointed to his job in spite of enormous opposition from politicians, newspapers, and the people in general, who saw Daugherty as a cheap and unreliable fixer. Daugherty's track record as a fixer, however, far from discrediting him, was precisely his main qualification for the job. Not all attorneys general are appointed for the same reason, but it is prudent for a president to have his chief law enforcement officer be someone who will see to it that the administration itself is not prosecuted for anything.

The attorney general's power derives not from his authority to prosecute criminals, but from his authority to decide which cases he will prosecute and which cases he will not prosecute or prosecute inadequately or let slide or quash, and in his authority to authorize an investigation or not, to promote an investigation or prevent it. It was this authority that brought bootleggers with cash to see Jess Smith–and that caused politicians with uncertain consciences to squirm when they considered Daugherty's wandering eye and erratic manner.

Will Hays, at five and a half feet, was the shortest man there, barely able to get his elbows up on the table. "He is the one hundred per cent American we have all heard so much talk about," the Washington journalist Edward Lowry said of him. "Apply any native or domestic standard and he complies with it to a hair-line. He is as indigenous as sassafras root. He is one of us. He is folks. . . . He is a human flivver, the most characteristic native product; a two-cylinder single-seater, good for more miles per gallon than any other make of man. He takes you there and brings you back . . . a politician to his finger-tips and a strong josher: a real handshaker and elbow massager."

Hays had been a precinct committeeman before he was twenty-one years old, and had been chairman of almost every Republican political committee Indiana had to offer before he became chairman of the National Republican Committee. He had been in nearly every factional fight in Indiana during the preceding twenty years and, as Lowry said, had "come through clean as a smelt." He was rewarded, and entrusted, with the job of postmaster general of the United States, the principal patronage dispenser of the federal government.

During the preceding administration, Wilson's Democratic administration, thirteen thousand Post Office jobs had been removed from the machinery of patronage and placed under nonpolitical Civil Service regulations. One of Harding's first acts as president was to return these jobs to the patronage dispensary. Newspaper editorial writers were appalled, but Hays disposed of the jobs with great finesse, according to the usages of honest corruption–that is, he did not simply give the jobs to loyal Republicans; rather he gave the jobs to loyal Republicans who could, and did, carry out their duties responsibly, giving almost a day's work for a day's pay. Newspaper editorial writers were relieved and grateful and praised Hays for not practicing politics with the Post Office.

John W. Weeks, secretary of war, sat to Hays's left at the table. Weeks was a plump, balding, boring man from Massachusetts who had been a member of the House of Representatives for eight years and then a senator and had, during his political career, built up his banking business back in Boston, so that he had become one of New England's leading bankers. In the convention of 1916, he had had a brief run at the Republican presidential nomination, and in the election of 1920, he had done some major fund raising for the party. He was a member in good standing of the Senate's Old Guard, although, because he had just lost in his bid for reelection to the Senate, he was available. He was Senator Lodge's choice. And he played poker.

Will Hays, postmaster general of the United States, dispensed patronage in the traditional Ohio manner of honest corruption, demanding almost a day's work for a full day's pay from nearly well-qualified loyal supporters.

As secretary of war, Weeks might have been expected to be interested in demobilizing the war machine that had been built up during World War I, or taking a profit from the sale of surplus military materials. In fact, he stepped delicately back from all these matters. The planning and construction of hospitals for veterans was transferred from the army to Harding's and Weeks's poker-playing friend Charlie Forbes at the Veterans' Bureau, and the disposal of surplus materials was transferred from the Quartermaster General's Department to Forbes's Veterans' Bureau, too. Weeks remained, like Hays, "clean as a smelt."

Edwin Denby, secretary of the navy, sat across the table from Hays. Denby was bullet-headed, thick jowled, with heavy lips and dull eyes; it was never clear whether he was bright or stupid. On the one hand, Denby had been quick witted enough to become a millionaire in the automobile business in Detroit and, when World War I broke out, to enlist as a private in the Marine Corps and rise through the ranks to major. But, when he ran into a spot of trouble during his term as secretary of the navy–because he had transferred some naval oil reserve lands from his jurisdiction to that of the Department of the Interior, which had turned them over to some private interests–he had such trouble remembering what he had done, such trouble recalling facts or understanding their significance, he betrayed such stupendous gullibility and absurd self-assurance, and he looked so dumb that he was finally accounted an honest but extraordinarily feeble-headed man. And so, as secretary of the navy, he would have, like Hays and Weeks, no blemish on his record–save, the perhaps undeserved, one of stupidity.

James Davis, secretary of labor, served his purpose merely by sitting at the cabinet table; indeed, the less he did to represent the interests of the workers, the better Harding liked it. Davis, a short, muscular, robust man, had been an ironworker who came up through the union ranks and, at the same time, came up through the ranks of the Loyal Order of Moose, with such cheerful success that he had been able to become a banker and a believer–because of his own experience of life–that any poor boy can make good and

Edwin W. Denby, secretary of the navy, was smarter than he looked: he signed naval oil reserves over to the Department of the Interior, so private oilmen could arrange with Interior to drill at Teapot Dome.

that the rich are rich because they work hard and deserve to be rich.

"When labor loafs," said Davis, "it injures labor first and capital last." He believed strikes were bad and that labor-management "cooperation" was good. Workers ought to accept wage cuts, he felt, to let management get the country back to prosperity.

He constantly wrote notes to Harding, little notes of praise about one thing or another that the president had done; and every time Davis made a speech or said something to a newspaper reporter—usually something gushingly favorable to Harding—a mimeographed copy of it would be delivered to the president. Harding liked him. "You have brought to the office," Harding once wrote Davis, "all that I have expected."

Henry Wallace, secretary of agriculture, who sat next to

Davis, chewed tobacco, as Harding did, but in very small, almost unnoticeable chaws: he did not move his jaws, and he did not spit, choosing instead, to swallow the juice. He had a round, pink face and wore pince-nez, and he liked to play golf. Harding liked to play with him, because Wallace shot in the eighties, and Harding always felt braced by the challenge.

Wallace was a moderate Progressive, the editor of a farm journal in Iowa, and he enjoyed enormous respect among farmers, conservationists, and Progressives around the country. Stubbornly independent, unwilling ever to compromise, a battler at the cabinet table for the rights and plight of farmers, a man with a disarming charm and a large repertory of Scottish jokes, Wallace stood up for his rural constituents with zealous honor.

Having gotten such a fine man in his cabinet–and enjoying the good will of the farmers for having done so–Harding could well afford to ignore Wallace all he liked. While the secretary of agriculture told the president that hundreds of thousands of farmers could not obtain credit, that the economy was being manipulated to their disadvantage, that they were overwhelmed with debt and unable, in many cases, to buy fertilizer, that they were the victims of an economic condition that they had not brought about, Harding explained to Wallace that "Government paternalism, whether applied to agriculture or to any other of our great national industries, would stifle ambition, impair efficiency, lessen production and make us a nation of dependent incompetents. . . . Every farm is an economic entity by itself. Every farmer is a captain of industry. The elimination of competition among them would be impossible without sacrificing that fine individualism that still keeps the farm the real reservoir from which the nation draws so many of the finest elements of its citizenship."

Albert Fall, secretary of the interior, had grown up in the farming country of Kentucky, an orphan, raised in poverty by a grandfather. Working his way out of Kentucky, he was a schoolteacher, bookkeeper, cattlehand, chuckwagon cook, miner, timberman, and mining foreman. He fetched up in Mexico at the age of nineteen, knowing a little about law, a little about mining, and a little Spanish, and put together a living by representing Spanish-speaking clients in cases involving mineral rights, land titles, and cattle rustling.

Out among the mines near Silver City, New Mexico, Fall met Edward Doheny, a broke prospector, and they became lifelong friends. Doheny found his way into the oil business, and Fall found his way into politics, in New Mexico, and then in the Senate, where he had sat at the desk just next to Harding's and became Harding's poker-playing chum. "The man's face," said William Allen White, "figure and mien were a shock to me . . . a tall, gaunt, unkempt, ill-visaged face that showed a disheveled spirit behind restless eyes. He looked like the patent medicine vender of my childhood days who used to stand, with long hair falling down upon a long coat under a wide hat, with military goatee and mustache, at the back of a wagon selling Wizard Oil."

He made no bones about his feelings for conservationists. The nation's resources were there to be exploited, and profits were meant to go to the quick and the shrewd. "His speech is fast," one of his opponents said, "his manner is impetuous, and he becomes instantly aggressive at opposition. At these times his powerful face clouds to sternness, he sits forward in his chair, and pounds his statements home with gesticulation; or throws his head back till he faces the ceiling while roaring with laughter at his opponents' replies. He does not argue, because he does not listen." Nothing in Fall's background or temperament would have prepared him to be naive or overly scrupulous or reluctant to seize on an opportunity or hesitant to expect a favor in return for a favor.

A man who moved as fast as Fall was bound to leave some loose ends, and at the time he joined Harding's cabinet, he was short of funds. He owned one of the largest ranches in New Mexico, a ranch scattered in various tracts in a stretch fifty-five miles long and twenty-four miles wide, and he had engaged in improvements and enlargements in his properties that had left him more than $140,000 in debt and eight years behind in taxes.

Andrew W. Mellon, the secretary of the treasury, who shook hands only with the tips of his fingers, impressed one reporter as "a tired double-entry bookkeeper who is afraid of losing his job." Mellon reduced the national debt to two-thirds of its former level and cut taxes for the rich, and so helped make the boom that led to the Crash.

It was to this man that Harding asked Denby to turn over, among other naval oil reserves, the reserves in California at Elk Hills and the reserves in Wyoming, about fifty miles north of Caspar, at Teapot Dome.

Andrew Mellon, the secretary of the treasury, who sat just to the left of Harding at the head of the table, "looks like a tired double-entry bookkeeper," Edward Lowry said, "who is afraid of losing his job. He gives the instant impression of being worn and tired, tired, tired. He is slight and frail. He sits in a chair utterly relaxed. He wears dark, sober clothes, a black tie, his coat always buttoned, and in these days, when even the office boys sport silk, his socks are black, cotton lisle, and not pulled up as sharply as they might be. . . . Sometimes in his office he smokes small black paper cigarettes. When they go out, he relights them and smokes them right down to the end. Not an eighth of an inch is wasted. He doesn't smoke lightly, casually, unconsciously, but precisely, carefully, consciously, as a man computing interest on $87.76 for two months and eight days at 4% per annum. Mr. Mellon looks as if he didn't know what fun was, and I don't believe he does. . . . When he shakes hands he gives you only the tips of his fingers."

The son of a wealthy Pittsburgh banker, Mellon had been banker to the robber barons and become, with Rockefeller and Ford, one of the three wealthiest men in America. His investments included steel, railroads, utilities, water power, distilleries, coal, oil, insurance, and aluminum.

At the level of a man such as Mellon, graft is elevated beyond common recognition, transmuted and dignified to the status of policy. In Mellon's view, the slumping postwar American economy needed protection from foreign competition so that it could get back on its feet, regain its vigor, and then go back out into the world. What was required was a tariff wall that would protect American farms and factories. Mellon's policy found its expression in the Fordney-McCumber Act of 1922, which established the highest tariff rates in American history. Incidentally, those who controlled the Mellon investments, for example, in aluminum, and thus the alumium market, immediately put up the price of aluminum behind the protective tariff barrier, and made an annual profit of $10 million on an investment of $18 million.

In Mellon's view, the wartime excess-profits tax needed to be repealed and the surtax on the rich needed to be cut from 65 percent to 50 percent, to put more capital into the hands of the rich and the corporations so that they could have more capital to invest. This policy, a form of "supply side economics," though a happy one for Mellon in the short run, was ultimately not widely admired. "This surplus capital," Andrew Sinclair said, "was, in turn, to find its way to the stock market and start the speculative boom that was to end in the Great Depression and in the fracture of the image of Mellon the great financier."

Herbert Hoover, who sat at the far end of the table to Harding's right, was the secretary of commerce. "Mr. Hoover's face," said Clinton Gilbert, one of the journalists who watched him over the years, "is not that a decisive character. The brow is ample and dominant; there is vision and keen intelligence; but the rest of the face is not strong, and it wears habitually a wavering self-conscious smile." He was an awkward man, uncomfortable in situations of fluidity or give-and-take. At the dinner table, he did not move easily in and out of a conversation but tended to keep his head buried in his plate until the conversation reached a topic about which he knew something; then he would look up, burst in with some relevant facts, and lapse again into silence. He rarely said anything bright or clever, but often sounded solid and reasonable. He was best, once he did get going, at monologues or lectures in which no one interrupted or questioned him. Once, playing with some small children, building a dam across a stream, Hoover was captivated with the task, wading into the water to fetch stones and filling in the chinks with clay; the children with whom he played, however, were most impressed that he played in the river "with all his clothes on."

The professional politicians detested Hoover. "Hoover gives most of us gooseflesh," Senator Brandegee said. No one could still be certain whether he was a Republican or a Democrat, that is to say, whether he would be a loyal party man and reward other loyal party men. His awkwardness was unsettling to the sort of men who liked to shake hands, slap backs, grab elbows, play poker, have a drink, and tell a joke. His standoffishness seemed suspicious, as though he might not be the sort of man who would, in a pinch, come through. All of the Old Guard in the Senate opposed Hoover.

For some reason, Harding insisted on having Hoover in the cabinet–because Hoover's name was so well known and so admired that Hoover would provide good window dressing for the cabinet or because Harding purposely wanted to defy the Senate's Old Guard and declare his independence or because Hoover provided a

Herbert Hoover, secretary of commerce, believed with some consistency that taxes should be cut, interest rates should be lowered, and people should fend for themselves—though banks needed federal aid.

voice in the cabinet for the West and the Far West or because Harding understand Hoover's economic views and plans and shared them.

In any case, when he was choosing his cabinet, Harding let it be known that he wanted Hoover, and the Old Guard let it be known that they could not tolerate him. The Old Guard did want Mellon, however: Mellon was the candidate of them all, and especially of Boss Penrose of Pennsylvania. And so Harding sent Daugherty to speak to Penrose, Knox, and Lodge. Harding would take "Mellon and Hoover," said Daugherty, "or no Mellon."

Penrose, said Daugherty, "rose to heights of profanity I have never heard equaled. He swore in every mood and tense. I had 'cussed' a little at times when unduly provoked. But I listened in awe to my master's voice." Penrose consented.

Hoover's policies as secretary of commerce appealed perfectly to Harding. To Hoover, the postwar economic slump, with its unemployment and its collapsing agricultural prices and industrial income and wages, was a good thing, "the result of inflation and disaster from the war," and a necessary adjustment. America had had fourteen depressions since the Civil War and had "come through the thirteen others all right." It did not seem possible to Hoover, Andrew Sinclair has written, "to doubt a system that had failed fourteen times in fifty-five years, although he would certainly have doubted a company that had done so once."

"There is always unemployment," Harding said, in agreement with Hoover. "Under most fortunate circumstances, I am told, there are a million and a half in the United States who are not at work. The figures are astounding only because we are a hundred millions, and this parasite percentage is always with us."

Hoover's notion was that there might be more "cooperation" between government and business, with government paving the way for entrepreneurs to make flourishing enterprises, helping businessmen instead of hindering them, opening up markets and opportunities. When he took over the Commerce Department, it was an undistinguished operation. His predecessor told him he would hardly have to work more than two hours a day, "putting the fish to bed at night and turning on the lights around the coast." But Hoover saw his department as America's leading business booster and he built his own empire in the Commerce Department to show just how it was done. He set up a Division of Housing in his department, charged to encourage more and more building of individual houses, to boom the sanctity of the single-family home, to work out credit facilities and to get rid of cumbersome state and municipal building regulations. He saw to it that his department's budget was increased by more than 50 percent; he added employees; and he set up statistical services and broadcast business information across the country. He acquired the Bureau of Custom Statistics from the Department of the Treasury and took over the Bureau of Mines and the Patent Office from Interior.

The key to his program for economic revival, however, was in his Bureau of Foreign and Domestic Commerce. The man who had been all around Europe organizing relief programs and had seen a great deal of European business at first hand understood that, at a certain point, economic policy rises naturally to a level of international arrangements.

He cleared out Wilson's appointees in the Commerce Department and replaced them with men who understood foreign languages, economics, and law. He set up trade offices in a number of major American and European cities; he quintupled the number of employees working in the foreign department, and he increased the budget for foreign operations from $860,000 to $5 million. It was Hoover who was the first to give a big, and concerted, official boost to the institution of the American multinational company and to American economic internationalism.

Immediately to Harding's right at the cabinet table sat the last of the cabinet members, the secretary of state, Charles Evans Hughes, "a bearded iceberg," as Teddy Roosevelt had called him. "He is as destitute of graces," Edward Lowry said, "of lights and shades, of frailties and foibles, of idiosyncrasies and little personal eccentricities, of the 'human interest' touch, as any man in public life."

He was reckoned a man of impeccable character, of absolute moral rectitude, a stiff figure. On the rare occasions, Lowry said, "when he tried to unbend he almost audibly creaked." A just man, an able man, he was regarded by some as a "Viking in a frock coat."

He had been a champion of public welfare, governor of New York, associate justice of the Supreme Court, a candidate for president in 1916, and he would be chief justice of the Supreme Court. "He had a trick," Lowry noticed, "of standing back flat on his heels. This made his shoes turn up at the toes so that from the ball of the foot forward the soles did not touch the ground. He made an impressive figure."

Charles Evans Hughes, secretary of state, redefined the foreign policy of the United States as one that would henceforth be characterized not by ideals or moral precepts but by the satisfaction of "interests."

In foreign relations, Harding was stuck with a country that had just repudiated President Wilson's League of Nations. Some said that the entire election had been nothing but a referendum on the League of Nations. The opposition to the league had been stated as worry that America would lose its historic character if it were to become entangled with evil and cynical Europeans. The essential concern was that foreign entanglements would lead to an internationalist, imperialist foreign policy, with all the customary damage that does to a democratic country: the flow of power out of state and local governments to the federal government, and, within the federal governments, to the executive branch, and within the executive branch into the hands of an imperial presidency and so ending in the destruction of the Republic itself. The question of internationalism versus isolationism had been drawn in no less compelling terms than these.

And yet, Harding had somehow straddled the issue during the election campaign. He was against Wilson's league, no doubt of that. He was against that sort of vague idealism that Wilson had come to represent. But he was not quite, altogether, against some sort of American role in the world. And, when it came time to choose his cabinet, Harding appointed both Hoover and Hughes, both of them well known as internationalists.

Just what Harding was about confused editorial writers, who resorted to commonplace political explanations: Harding wanted to make peace with the liberal wing of the party; Harding wanted to smooth over differences; Harding wanted to blunt criticism by absorbing it.

But Hughes made the difference between Wilson and Harding clear: Hughes spoke, on behalf of the new administration, in terms not of American "ideals," but of American "interests." America would enter the world to pursue its interests—that and that alone. No one could object to that. To protect one's own interests was surely an unimpeachable intent. To pursue one's natural interest is simply to be true to one's character to pursue one's natural destiny.

Harding's cabinet, said William Allen White, "looked to me like a lot of pallbearers who never once got down to the truth about the deceased." They were (seated, left to right) Secretary of War John W. Weeks, Andrew Mellon, Charles Evans Hughes, Harding, Vice President Calvin Coolidge, Edwin Denby, and (standing, left to right) Secretary of the Interior Albert Fall, Will Hays, Attorney General Harry Daugherty, Secretary of Agriculture Henry Wallace, Herbert Hoover, and Secretary of Labor James W. Davis.

America's destiny, as Hughes understood it, harmonized nicely with Hoover's and Harding's views. "The policy of the Government with relation to foreign investments should be well understood. . . . [It] is the policy of the open door. We seek equality of opportunity for our nationals. We do not attempt to make contracts for them. . . . We do not favor one of our nationals as against another. Given the open door, all who wish are entitled to walk in. We resist policies of discrimination against American capital. This is true whether it relates to oil or telegraphs."

In short, the destiny of America was not essentially to be a bastion of liberty and justice, but rather a machine for making money. It was a view with which Mellon and Fall, Wallace and Davis, Denby and Weeks, Hays and Daugherty and Jess Smith could all agree. From this, all else would follow.

XXI. Bribery

WHEN THE UNITED States entered World War I, the American government took over all the property in the United States that was owned by Germans. One such piece of property was the American Metal Company, owned by the Metallgesellschaft and Metall Bank of Frankfort-on-Main, Germany. The American government took over the company, sold it, and invested the income in Liberty Bonds. By 1921, these bonds, with accumulated interest, were worth $6,500,000.

The original owners of the American Metal Company, in an attempt to get their investment back, claimed that it had not been owned by Germans at all—and so had been incorrectly taken over. It had really belonged all along to some Swiss investors, the Société Suisse pour Valeurs de Métaux.

Whatever the merits of the claim, a German attorney named Richard Merton arrived in New York to see whether he could not find an American lawyer "who could pave the way" and get some "speed" in the Office of the Alien Property Custodian in Washington. Merton found his way to John T. King, a Bridgeport garbage collector who had been General Leonard Wood's campaign manager until Wood fired him for being too familiar with the bosses. King was, said Mark Sullivan, "a 'smoothie,' suave, soft-spoken, well-dressed. . . . He was unobtrusive in manner but energetic in action, slow in speech but quick in mind, always a formidable combination."

The procedure in this case, as in many thousands of others involving hundreds of millions of dollars, was to present the claimant's argument to the Alien Property Custodian and then, to make certain that there was no corruption or illegality involved, to have the custodian's judgment in the case taken to the office of the attorney general for confirmation. "In this case," Samuel Hopkins Adams said of the procedure, "it was expedited, in fact 'greased.' "

The custodian was Colonel Thomas Miller, "a lawyer of good though not eminent standing," as Adams said, "a Yale graduate, a communicant of the Episcopal Church, a member of leading Philadelphia clubs, a man of unblemished character and record, he might have stood as the type of the gentleman in politics."

Merton filed his claim on September 20, 1921. The claim was approved and forwarded to the attorney general on September 22. The papers were returned, approved, on September 23. Miller was able, within a few days, to give Merton a Treasury check for $6,453,979.97, and two packages of Liberty Bonds worth $514,350. Merton was naturally pleased and gave an intimate celebratory dinner in New York for Miller, John King, and Jess Smith. He had a small token of his appreciation for all who had helped him: a handsome $200 cigarette case for each of them. As an additional token of his appreciation, he gave $441,000 worth of Liberty Bonds to John King, of which King gave $50,000 worth to Colonel Miller, kept $112,000 for himself, gave a double share of $224,000 worth to Jess Smith, and somehow disposed of another $55,300 worth in a way that has never yet been traced.

XXII.

Corruption

"MY DEAR JOHN," Charles Hayden, of Hayden, Stone & Company of Boston, wrote to Secretary of War John Weeks:

> Ordinarily I would hate to bring these matters to your personal attention, but the way the general situation has been developing in the last six months it seems to me that everything that can be done by co-operation between bankers and the Government to inspire confidence in a legitimate way should be done, and that is why I feel a perfectly clear conscience in giving you this little additional bother.

The bother of which Hayden spoke was a claim that the government had against the Wright-Martin Aircraft Company, of which Hayden happened to be a director, for receiving $5,267,467.75

more than it should have during the war in payment for Hispano-Suiza airplane motors. Weeks, the former Bostonian, replied:

> My Dear Hayden:
>
> In view of the steps that have already been taken, I am convinced that the proper procedure is for the company to come in before the Air Service section and make their showing.
>
> Whatever decision may be reached by the Air Service section you should understand is not conclusive. Not only is the approval of a higher officer required, but even if that approval is obtained, there is a further appeal to myself.

Secretary of War Weeks was not indicted.

XXIII.

Bribery and Corruption

ON THE FOURTH of July 1921, Ned McLean gave a party at his house on I Street for President and Mrs. Harding, Secretary of State Hughes, Daugherty, several ambassadors, and a crowd of senators and representatives. The I Street house was a grand pile, occupying half a block, with a ballroom that could accommodate several dining tables, each a hundred feet long, and with a living room that, at Christmastime, had ample space for a three-story-high Christmas tree. Barberini tapestries decorated the walls of the ballroom, and Evalyn Walsh McLean liked to have masses of flowers about the house.

The high point of the party was the screening of a movie that had been rushed to Washington by one of Ned's functionaries, Jap Muma—a movie of the prize fight that had been held two days before at Boyle's Thirty Acres in New Jersey between Jack Dempsey, then the heavyweight champion of the world, and the French contender Georges Carpentier. Dempsey won by a knockout, and the guests were wonderfully enthusiastic about the film. In the chitchat that followed, someone mentioned that it was too bad that people all over the United States could not see the movie.

In fact, it had been illegal for McLean to have the film. Almost a dozen years before, when the black fighter Jack Johnson beat the white fighter Jim Jeffries, a law was passed to prohibit the

Jack Dempsey, in the dark trunks, beat Georges Carpentier in the fourth round of their heavyweight bout for the world championship—and Jess and the boys put in the fix to profit on illegal films of the fight.

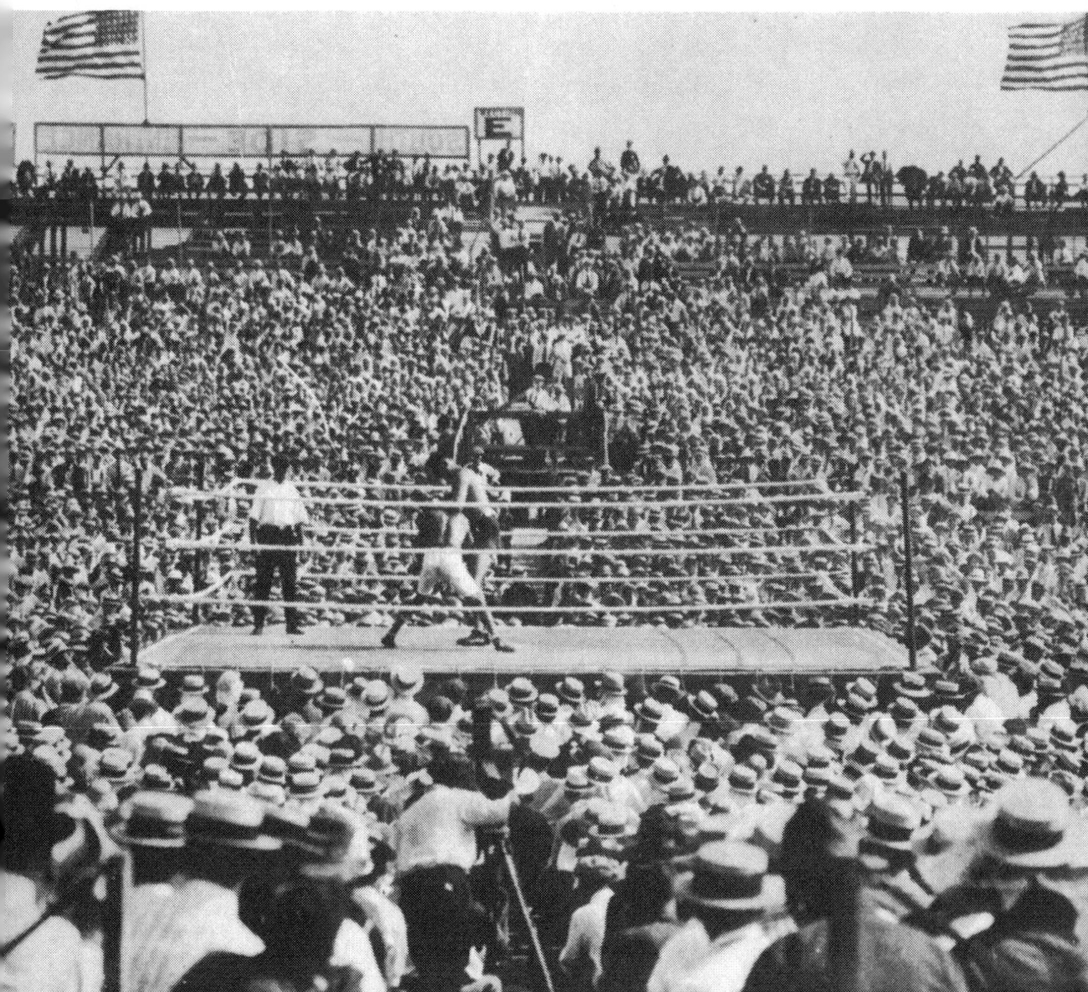

transportation of fight films across state lines—to prevent the "humiliating spectacle of a white man beaten by a negro" from getting around. Daugherty, always quick to spot a loophole, remarked that the law only prohibited the transportation of films; it did not prohibit their exhibition once they had gotten across the state lines. He told Jap Muma that Muma should get hold of an old friend of Daugherty's from Ohio, Alfred Urion, "one of the greatest little men you ever met in your life." Muma and Urion ought to be able to work something out, Daugherty thought, and "if you put this across," he said to Muma, "you ought to get a big cut—not less than fifty per cent."

The idea Urion and Muma worked out was simple. Urion came up with the names of some lawyer friends in the states where the film could be shown for a good profit. These men would take the rap for bringing the film across state lines. It would be fixed that each of these men would then be fined the lowest possible amount, and then the movies could be shown. They would be shown first, for free, to an American Legion audience, or some war veterans' organization. Then, it would be arranged to have some newspaper reporters alerted so that they could raise a stink in their papers against the ban on the film. Then the film would be released.

In New York, it was arranged to show the film first at a hospital for disabled soldiers on Staten Island. (William Orr was able to lend a hand for the arrangements in New York, for which he took a 20 percent cut.) The United States attorney in New York then prosecuted the makers of the film and fined them $1,000 each. Newspapers printed editorials in favor of showing the movie (Orr's old contacts with newsmen helped in this). Then the movie was released. It turned a quick profit in New York of $75,000, and went from there to twenty-one states, making a profit, altogether, of about a million dollars.

Jess Smith Returns to Washington Court House

ONCE EVERY TWO or three weeks, Jess Smith would board the train with his two heavy black leather suitcases for the long trip back to Washington Court House. He carried no money in his suitcases: they were filled with his clothes and bottles of bootleg liquor for his personal use. He carried the money, and sometimes stocks or bonds, in a money belt around his waist, sometimes as much as $75,000 in thousand dollar bills.

Roxy waited for him faithfully in Washington Court House, and whenever he hit town, he had a bottle of whiskey for her and some hundred dollar bills or some five hundred dollar bills. Sometimes he gave her some shares of stock, some White Motors stock, or some Beaman G. Dawes Pure Oil Company stock; sometimes he gave her candy or flowers, and they often went on long rides together just as though they were courting.

The gossips of Washington Court House did not lack for

subject matter when it came to discussing the independent ways of Roxy Stinson-Smith-Stinson, and, among other things, they marveled at the utter faithfulness of Jess and Roxy toward one another.

Jess told Roxy of "the doings in Washington," as she called them, and especially of stories about his friend Harry Daugherty. Harry was "the first thing we talked about," Roxy said, "and the last thing. . . . Jess Smith was a great admirer of Harry Daugherty all his life long. I think he was his ideal."

Jess took the money along to Mally Daugherty, Harry's brother, who had become something of a community leader in Washington Court House. He was a tall, strongly built man, with enormous vitality, and an ability to work long hours that impressed all his fellow townspeople. He never left Washington Court House; he married a girl from the town; and he enjoyed the confidence of his neighbors. He often pitched into community enterprises, taking on the duties of chairman of one civic cause or another. During the war, he had been chairman of the Fayette County War Chest and had whooped it up with gusto, never failing to meet the county's quota for Liberty Bonds–and naturally feeling appreciative when the local draft board found it did not need to call his son to active service. Jess put the money in Mally's bank.

As Jess squired Roxy around the hometown, he loved to tell her about where he had been with "Warren" (he dropped the president's first name every chance he got, in New York, in Washington, in Washington Court House, even with Roxy), and what sort of deals were going on. He told her how he had been asked to join the Metropolitan Club in Washington, how he was listed in the *Social Register* now, how he had an office right in the Justice Department, how senators called him "Mister," how people came to him begging favors, how he and Harry kept a ticker-tape machine right there in the Justice Department, and how Jess would follow the market, take the latest quotations into Harry's office, where they would decide to put some money into one stock or another. As one of the members of the Ohio gang is rumored to have grumbled, "She knows enough to hang us all."

Jess Smith wears a Chesterfield coat and an expression worthy of one who bears the heavy burdens of state. (Historical Pictures Service, Inc., Chicago)

Jess loved the excitement of Washington. He would stand, Mark Sullivan said, "on the curb of what was then one of the great crossroads of Washington, the corner of Fifteenth and H streets, location of the old Shoreham Hotel; two blocks to the south the White House, with Harding in it; one block to the north the Department of Justice, with Harry Daugherty presiding. Smith would stand on the Shoreham corner, his head up, his features eager and happy, his coat lapels spread back, his thumbs in the armholes of his vest. To an acquaintance across the street he would call, 'Hey there, come on over.' Always his greeting was the same, 'What d'you know?' "

Roxy could tell for herself that Harry had come to depend on Jess. If Jess lingered too long in Washington Court House, Harry would begin to send telegrams asking him to come back, saying that he missed Jess and needed him. Harry had trouble sleeping without Jess in the same room–just as Jess had trouble sleeping unless someone were in the same room with him. Roxy sometimes resented having Jess's attention taken from her, but she understood. "They lived together," she said. "They were intimate friends, and Jess adored him. . . . He lived for him, he loved him. He had not been in Washington more than three or four months until he said, 'I am not made for this. This intrigue is getting me crazy. If I could just come home, but I am in now and I have to stand by Harry.' "

Just what Jess was "in" he sometimes did not exactly say. He could be evasive, or barely suggestive, at times. Sometimes he seemed nervous, even somewhat frightened, by the deals he was in, but it was too late to turn back, even if he had brought himself to think about turning back. Whatever he was in, he was in over his head.

On one of Jess's visits to Ohio, in the lobby of the Hotel Deschler, he paused to say hello to George Remus, a Cincinnati pharmacist who was known as "the King of the Bootleggers."

XXV.

The King of the Bootleggers

George Remus had grown up on the northwest side of Chicago where, when his father was taken ill, he went to work at the age of fourteen for an uncle who owned a drugstore. George was a stocky, muscular boy, a fast talker who spoke with a trace of a German accent and who tended to use words that were a little longer than he could comfortably pronounce or smoothly work into his sentences. He was a bright boy, though, and within five years he had managed to buy his uncle's drugstore. During the next five years he bought a second drugstore, acquired a pharmacist's license, an optometrist's certificate, had an affair with a customer, married her, had a child with her, attended night school, and became a lawyer. By 1920, he was making $50,000 a year as a criminal lawyer, having an affair with a young divorcée named Imogene who worked in his office, and looking around for something else to do.

Several of his clients, taking advantage of the laws that had been passed recently in Congress, were bootleggers, and Remus figured that if they were smart enough to make small fortunes, then he was smart enough to make a big fortune. Nor did Remus have any moral objections to alcohol or to getting around a law he considered foolish, although he was himself a teetotaler.

Remus understood the law, and he understood the drugstore business; so he understood at once how to obey the law to the letter in buying and selling liquor for medicinal purposes. He also saw that a number of slow-witted distillery owners did not understand how to get around the Prohibition laws, and that he could buy their distilleries at bargain prices. He would then be both seller and buyer.

"He had calculated," according to Thomas Coffey, "that 80 percent of the bonded whiskey in the United States was stored in government-controlled warehouses within three hundred miles" of Cincinnati. And so he divorced his wife, married Imogene, and moved with Imogene and her daughter by a previous marriage to Cincinnati. He was wild about Imogene, and she was in love with him. They worked together in their new business, and they made money faster than they could properly keep track of it. Remus had saved up $100,000, and he put $10,000 down on a distillery and deposited the rest in the Lincoln National Bank, to impress the bankers with his resources. Within four months, with bank financing, he was in the drug business, had formed a few corporations to receive the liquor his distilleries would sell, had bought a ten-acre estate, was negotiating for the purchase of several more distilleries, and had invited forty-four men to his office one day–including politicians, Prohibition agents, and federal marshals–and had given each of them an average of $1,000 as an introduction to his friendship.

By the end of the year, he owned stills in Ohio, Kentucky, and Indiana. He had hundreds of employees, still workers, truck drivers, armed guards for his trucks, people to manage a bottling works and storage facility at Death Valley Farm, northwest of Cincinnati. He was in a business whose bookkeeping was necessarily so sketchy that he had to keep track of the operation in his head, and the business was expanding so rapidly that he could only estimate the total volume. In his first year, he moved perhaps three quarters of a million gallons of liquor. Altogether, he was embarked on an enterprise that would gross something on the order of $50 million.

He bought some of his permits from Jess Smith, meeting Jess from time to time—at the Deschler Hotel in Columbus, at the Commodore or the Plaza in New York, at the Claypool in Indianapolis. He could not remember just how many permits he got from Jess, but he figured Jess must have given him permits for at least 250,000 cases, paid for on a sliding scale of $1.50 to $2.50 per case, roughly $500,000 at a minimum.

Remus made only one mistake. Impatient with all the government red tape, he went ahead and released some liquor from his warehouses without benefit of permits. Realizing that he was risking a different sort of trouble for this activity, and for general purposes of protection, he made another deal with Jess Smith—entirely apart from his payments for permits. For occasional payments of $50,000, which added up over a period of time to an additional $250,000 or $300,000, Remus bought immunity from prosecution. He might be bothered by a naive Prohibition agent from time to time, but he need not worry. If a charge led to an indictment, the fix was in. Remus hadn't a worry in the world.

XXVI.

Bribery and Corruption and Sex and Suicide

CHARLIE FORBES HAD met Harding in 1915, in Hawaii, where Forbes was overseeing the construction of the Pearl Harbor naval base and Harding was passing through on a Senate junket. Forbes had "every needful quality," said Samuel Hopkins Adams, "of the universal good fellow and high-class confidence man." He was a pink, round-faced, redheaded, cherubic sort of a fellow—"breezy," said Mark Sullivan, "joke-cracking, hustling"—who wore bow ties and practiced the arts of flirtation, flattery, and seduction with the offhand dedication of a natural athlete.

He took the Hardings out to see the sights in Hawaii, and called on them, too, with ingratiating frequency, lavish with his time and attentions and considerateness. He was a shrewd poker player. He loved to bet at cards and dice, and he won or lost with equal joviality. He loved to sit with a drink in his hand and tell a story, or hear one. He would roll in genially, with a boisterous greeting, and throw himself at a chair, saying, "Hello, Duchess. What about a little drink for a thirsty hombre?" He did not neglect to make frequent passes at Mrs. Harding, which may have been a unique experience for her, and she liked him. So did Harding. They both felt grateful to him and buoyed up by his presence.

When Harding took office as president, he called his chum Forbes to Washington to take over the Veterans' Bureau—a department that had control of the construction of hospitals for veterans, and also of the purchase and disposing of hospital supplies. Although the Veterans' Bureau did not sound like a very grand operation, Forbes's bureau made some of the cabinet offices look trivial by comparison: he had 30,000 jobs at his disposal, and a budget of $500 million a year. Indeed, the jobs and budget grew as the bureau found more and more veterans to care for; in no time, it was discovered that patients were being encouraged to stay on in hospitals after they had been cured; a third of the patients at the tuberculosis hospital in Greenville, South Carolina, were not suffering from tuberculosis at all, and, at the Speedway Hospital in Chicago, 80 percent of the patients spent most of their time on the town.

Because the veterans' hospitals were so overcrowded, it was essential to build more hospitals at once, and so Forbes turned immediately to the urgent need to let contracts to construction companies.

It happened that, in the course of ingratiating himself with Harding, Forbes had met Harding's sister, Mrs. Carolyn Votaw, the wife of a Seventh Day Adventist minister whom Harding had absent-mindedly appointed superintendent of federal prisons. As a matter of course, Forbes practiced his flirting on Carolyn—and she fell for him. Just how far she fell is not clear—she was, like her husband, a serious Adventist—but she responded to Forbes sufficiently that the Reverend Votaw threatened once to throw Forbes out a window.

Carolyn introduced Forbes to some acquaintances of hers, Elias and Kate Mortimer, an attractive young couple; and Carolyn and Charlie, Mort (Elias) and Kate took to spending a lot of time

Charlie Forbes, who flattered and charmed, loved to laugh, and seemed sincere, almost got away with it.

together on the town. Charlie loved to throw expensive dinner parties in Washington restaurants–Carolyn and Kate and Mort had never had such extravagant fun–and, occasionally, when the mood took him, he loved a big weekend party–taking half a floor in an Atlantic City hotel, say, and inviting a crowd of Broadway stars and other celebrities to come down to the resort for the weekend and dine and party day and night.

He did not neglect to pay attention to Kate, either, and even to find a job for her brother in the Veterans' Bureau, and Kate, like

Carolyn, could not help responding to his daring and his compliments. As for Mort, who happened to be a representative for the Thompson-Black construction companies, Forbes hinted broadly that, although he had to open up the hospital construction business to competitve bidding, he could always give a friend an advance look at a potential site so the friend could get in a really carefully prepared bid. For that matter, if all else failed, Forbes could always open up the sealed bids he got and let his friends know just what sort of bid they needed to submit in order to win.

Mortimer thought it would be a lot of fun to take a trip across country with Forbes (Mort would pick up all the checks) and look over some of these potential hospital sites. So Mort and Kate and Charlie set out together. Forbes left Carolyn behind. It was his biggest mistake.

They stopped in Chicago first, where they were meant to look over a site for a $5 million hospital, but they hardly had time to leave their suite at the Drake Hotel. It was such a comfortable set of rooms, and there was never a shortage of ice, or liquor, and they usually had five or ten people over for lunch or dinner, and the afternoons passed in continuous partying. Forbes could finish a quart of gin at a single sitting, and often did, and loved to sit and talk of deals, of what he could put over, and how there would be more than enough in it for everyone, and how he thought the future would be even more wonderful than the past. He said (this was confidential) that once he had put in his stint at the bureau, he was going to take over the Department of the Interior, and then there would be even more and better deals for everyone.

He could talk a happy prospect, he could conjure deals worth millions over half a bottle of scotch or gin, he could hint vaguely of what might be done with the $5 million worth of narcotics in the Veterans' Bureau warehouses or talk fondly of a project to rent a farm (with a $15,000 kickback) where veterans could be taught agriculture (and Forbes could give the farmer's wife a job in the bureau), for he liked to talk about the veterans, too, and what he and his friends would do for the veterans, and of how no one loved the veterans as much as he did. He could also digress on the pleasures of duck hunting or recall what a wonderful man the president was or he could rise to give an after-dinner speech and be filled suddenly with a generous emotion and pull some old inaugural medals out of his pocket (he had somehow got hold of a lot of them) and present one to some astonished man with a personal testimonial message from the president himself (which Forbes would improvise on the spot). He could weep at times, and at times he could bully, and sometimes, when the whim would overcome him, he could flare up when a man offered him a "commission," and declare with pure and righteous anger that he stood "for no graft." He had dignity and, at times, a lofty moral sensibility.

One afternoon, Mort returned to the suite at 4:30 to find Forbes and Kate in one of the bedrooms, on the bed together—shooting craps. Forbes had his coat off and a bottle of scotch at hand, and he was in a fine mood, having won $220 from Kate.

Fifteen or twenty people were out in the living room, including J. W. Thompson of the Thompson-Black construction company. Forbes had mentioned to Mort (who was picking up all the bills for their trip) that the cash was running low, and Mort took this occasion to have a chat with Thompson in the bathroom. Thompson gave Mort ten $500 bills, and Mort called Forbes into the bathroom and passed the money along.

By the time they had reached the West Coast, Forbes had gotten perhaps another $25,000 from the Thompson-Black company—and he and Mort were having squabbles about Mort's wife. One of Mort's employers told Mort not to get upset and spoil a good deal for everyone. Thompson, Mort, and Forbes came to a rough outline of a deal whereby Thompson would add $150,000 to each bid he made for a hospital and give Forbes $50,000 of it. In Spokane, Mort and Forbes met with a man named Hurley and took a walk by a lake, where they agreed that profits would be split three ways: one-third to Forbes, one-third to Hurley, and one-third to the Thompson-Black group.

He also laid on some side deals along the way. In Missouri, Forbes had agreed to buy a hospital site worth $35,000 for $77,000–and then insisted on renegotiating to raise the price to $90,000. In California, Forbes found a piece of land that an acquaintance had bought for $19,257. Forbes paid $105,000, with an understanding that he would take a $25,000 kickback.

Still, Mort was not happy with Forbes. Kate was too often found alone in hotel rooms with Forbes to keep explaining it away. By the time they had closed their deals on the West Coast and headed back for Washington, Mort was in a vengeful rage, Kate was talking of a separation, and Forbes had lost patience with Mort and had taken a moral position, telling everyone he would not do business with any firm that Mortimer represented. But worst of all for Forbes, Carolyn Votaw had kept track of all his movements on the trip.

Troubles never preyed for long on Forbes's mind, however. Back in Washington, he had plenty of business to attend to, including the question of what to do with the contents of the supply depot at Perryville, Maryland, which consisted of fifty separate buildings, crammed full of sheets, towels, liquor, drugs, gauze, pajamas, paper, thread, monkey wrenches, grindstones, and hundreds of old trucks.

In order to sell any of the stuff as unnecessary war surplus, Forbes had to draw up a list of the goods he meant to sell and show the list to the coordinator of the budget, a Colonel Smithers. Forbes sent such a list to Colonel Smithers one day, itemizing those goods that Forbes said were damaged or spoiled and that he would like to clear out of the warehouses. Smithers approved the list in a few minutes as a matter of course (except the soap, saying that the army and navy could always find use for soap), and returned it to Forbes. When the list came back to Forbes, he attached two more lists to it–amounting to more than three times the length of the original list–and the next day he sold it all to some friends: 84,920 bed sheets, 72,000 of them brand-new, in unopened packages, bought for $1 each, sold for 20 cents apiece; 1,169,800 towels that had cost 54 cents each, sold for 3 cents apiece; 98,995 pairs of pajamas made by women for the Red Cross and given to the army, sold for 30 cents apiece; 47,175 packages of gauze, sold at 20 percent of cost; 5,387 pounds of paraffin paper bought for 60 cents a pound, sold for 5 cents a pound; thread bought for $1.05 a pound, sold for 21 cents a pound. Altogether, for supplies worth between five and seven million dollars, Forbes's friends paid $600,000. They took it away as fast as possible, in 155 freight cars.

While Forbes was selling these items from the warehouses, he was buying more gauze, and paying $1.03½ each for new sheets. He not only replenished the stores he had depleted, however; he also looked around the warehouses and noted which items were entirely lacking. Among other things, he bought 35,035 gallons of floor cleaner and 32,115 gallons of floor wax (worth 1.8 cents per gallon) for 87 cents a gallon, a supply sufficient to last a hundred years.

"You are missing the *real old* times," one of Forbes's employees, who was out selling some bureau property, wrote to a friend back at the Wasnington office. "Hunting season is on–rabbit dinners, pheasant suppers, wines, beers, booze–and by God we haven't missed a one yet. . . . Oh, Boy! . . . we eat and wine with the mayor, the sheriff, the prosecuting atty. To hell with the Central Office and the work . . . the fun is in the field. . . . Let me know when Forbes is going to sell by sealed proposals, then's when I get a Rolls-Royce."

Carolyn Votaw no longer found Forbes so amusing. His trip west with the Mortimers had finished him with her, and when she heard of the doings at Perryville, she went to the Harding's old family doctor, Charlie Sawyer–who, because the president had appointed him surgeon general of the United States, shared some responsibility for the care of veterans. Mortimer told Sawyer about the storage depot, and Sawyer went to Harding.

At first, Harding refused to hear anything bad of Forbes, but when the magnitude of the graft finally made an impression on him and it was clear that he had only heard of a small part of Forbes's activities, he panicked. He got Forbes into his office, put him up against the wall, took him by the neck, and shook him–shouting "You yellow rat! You double-crossing bastard!"–and quickly sent him off on a mission to Europe to get him out of the country and cover up the story.

The embarrassment of the Veterans' Bureau could not be so easily buried, however. The newspapers learned of it, and Congress decided to look into it. Then the story was given renewed attention when one of Forbes's aides, a lawyer named Charles F. Cramer, proved unable to arrange things comfortably in his mind. Anticipating the charges that would ultimately touch on his reputation, and having a well-trained lawyer's exact understanding of the meaning of the charges, Cramer locked himself in the bathroom of his house and put a bullet through his head.

XXVII.

More of the Same with the Jap and Harry Mingle

AT THE END of the war, the Standard Aircraft Company and the Standard Aero Company found that they had received from the government $16,416,680.15 as part of the American effort to produce fighting planes to send to France. No American plane ever reached France during the war, and the two Standard companies could not account at all for $9,948,028.42 of the money they had received from the government. The Standard Aero Company went into bankruptcy, and the Standard Aircraft Company was liquidated after handing over some of its assets to Mitsui and Company. Mitsui and Company had owned and financed the two Standard companies through an American named Harry Mingle.

By the time Daugherty arrived at the Department of Justice, his department had been left with the job of collecting the sum of $2,267,342.75 from the Standard Aircraft Corporation—which was the largest amount that Justice Department attorneys had determined they could get back. Mitsui, meanwhile, decided to cut its losses and pay a bribe to stop the Justice Department suit.

Gaston Means had several techniques for collecting bribe money. His favorite was to rent a couple of adjoining rooms at the Vanderbilt Hotel in New York and put a large glass fishbowl in the middle of one room, station himself in the adjoining room, and watch the bowl through a peephole. Purchasers of favors would leave their money in the bowl and depart, never seeing Means.

For the Mitsui bribe, however, Means simply waited in a room at the Bellevue Hotel in Washington. "A Jap," he said, stepped into the room, handed him one hundred $1,000 bills, and left. Means gave the $100,000 to Jess Smith, and the Justice Department dropped the case.

Some time later, it was difficult to trace just who had agreed to what with whom, for Mitsui's man, Harry Mingle, was found dead in New York City.

The Big Oil Rip-Off And the Even Bigger One that Got Away

ON NEW YEAR'S Eve, the last day of 1921, Harry F. Sinclair arrived aboard his private railroad car, The Sinco, to visit with Secretary of the Interior Albert Fall at his Three Rivers Ranch in New Mexico. Sinclair had brought his lawyer, Colonel J. W. Zevely, and each had brought his wife. Fall met them at the branch-line Three Rivers station. There was no town, only a station, and the whole spread seemed somewhat down-at-heel and dustblown. Not long before, when another visitor had arrived at the ranch, he said that Fall owned a Franklin car "that we had to get out and fix three or four times to get 3 or 4 miles up to his house . . . [on] a very inferior, winding road, unmade road, and very rough." The ranch was vast, composed of prize lands, but the fences had gone unrepaired, the house was dilapidated, and the gossip in that part of the country was that Fall had not paid his taxes since 1912 and that he was broke.

Fall was ill, too. He suffered from chronic bronchial problems and pleurisy and arthritis, and not long before, he had been gored by a pet stag he had on his ranch. Two of his four children had died in the influenza epidemic of 1918; he had told his wife just before the 1920 Republican convention that he was disgusted with politics and wanted to get out. But he planned to leave his ranch to his children, and he wanted it to be in good repair and free of debt; so he held on a while longer until Three Rivers Ranch could be handed over to his children intact.

Harry Sinclair, bald, with bulging, froglike eyes, had started his business career as a drugstore clerk. He had grown up in Kansas and inherited a small sum of money when his father, the drugstore owner, died. He used that small stake to invest in options in the new Kansas oil fields. He bought his first oil well in 1905, and by 1915, he had become one of the biggest operators in Kansas. By 1920, he was one of the richest oilmen in the world.

Sinclair and his party stayed at Fall's ranch for three days. They slept aboard The Sinco, and they spent their days hunting deer and quail with the ranch hands and their evenings sitting before the fire in the main ranch house, talking oil.

The situation was this: in 1909 and 1910, President William Howard Taft had begun to take over certain tracts of land that were in the public domain and that appeared to hold oil, to keep them from private prospectors, and to reserve them for the future use of the navy. By the beginning of World War I, an eighth of all the oil lands in the United States had been reserved for possible military needs—and had become a bone of contention between navy men and oil men.

Three Rivers, said Fall, as he strolled about the ranch with his foreman and Harry Sinclair, was short of milch cows. Sinclair spoke up at once to say that he had far more blooded Holsteins on his own ranch than he really needed (and he made it a point to remember, after he returned home, to send six heifers, one yearling bull, two 6-month-old boars, and four young sows—along with an English racehorse for the foreman—over to Three Rivers Ranch). A

Albert B. Fall, the interior secretary with the visage of a riverboat gambler, plunged for bigger stakes, and lost.

few cows did not constitute a bribe worth millions of dollars in oil, but they did break the ice.

Sinclair was hardly the only fellow interested in oil. One of Fall's oldest friends, dating back to his prospecting days in New Mexico, was Edward Doheny, a little, meek-looking man with wire-rimmed glasses down on his nose and a large, sad, white walrus mustache. He had been a fruit packer, a mule driver, a waiter. He had fought off a mountain lion with a knife. He had fallen down a mine shaft and broken both legs, and while he had recuperated, he had studied the law. He was worth at least a hundred million dollars, and he had a yacht, and a fine home in California. Aside from the yacht and the home, however, Doheny lived a simple life; he seemed not so much a businessman as a wandering Celtic misfit lost in some private dream.

The trick about making a deal with Sinclair or Doheny on any of the government oil reserves was that, if a private operator were given the right to drill on navy reserves, as some private operators had been permitted to do on a limited basis in the past, he would have to pay a royalty to the government. The royalty payment would go directly to the Treasury. In this way, however, the navy got nothing out of its oil—so the navy opposed any deals on oil, saying that they were harmful to the national security.

Fall's stroke of genius was to figure a way to get the navy on his side. The navy, Fall realized, did not have as much oil as it thought it should have already pumped out of the ground and ready for use in storage tanks. Fall's idea was simple: private operators would drill on navy lands, but they would pay their royalties not in money—which would go to the Treasury—but in certificates that the navy could exchange for oil and for oil storage tanks. Thus the navy would get something out of the deal and support it.

All that stood in Fall's way then was the need for him to open the oil lands to competitive bidding. Fall reasoned, however, that

Harry Sinclair, the smiling oilman, did get away with it, for a while.

competitive bidding would force the United States to disclose its plans to build storage tanks: this information would be helpful to a potential enemy; thus, to open the bidding to competition would be to endanger the national security. Surely it was in the nation's interest to make a quiet deal.

With Doheny, Fall worked out a deal whereby Doheny's Pan American Petroleum and Transport Company would build storage tanks at Pearl Harbor, in Hawaii, and would be paid for the job with a grant of drilling rights at Reserve Number 1 in Elks Hill, California. The deal with Sinclair was a variation on the same theme. Sinclair got some reserves near Casper, Wyoming, the reserves that took their name from the eroded sandstone formation that sat atop the dome of oil like an inverted teapot–Teapot Dome.

Doheny's lawyers drew up a formal agreement incorporating Doheny's understanding with Fall and submitted a proposal to the Department of the Interior. Coincidentally, the day after the department received Doheny's proposal, Fall telephoned Doheny to say that he was "prepared now to receive that loan" that they had once casually mentioned in their conversation. On the following day, Doheny's son, Edward, Jr., withdrew $100,000 from the Doheny accounts at the brokerage house of Clair Company, wrapped the bills in paper, put them in a little black satchel, and took them over to Fall at his suite in Washington's Wardman Park Hotel.

The next week, Fall took the cash with him to Three Rivers. There, for $91,500, he bought the neighboring, 3,000 acre Harris Ranch. The Harris Ranch controlled the headwaters of the Three Rivers Canyon, and thus controlled the source of much of Fall's water for his ranch. With this purchase, he had bought a crucial measure of security for his children; and so it was that his first money went into the Harris Ranch acquisition.

From Sinclair, Fall received $198,000 in Liberty Bonds, then another $35,000 worth of bonds, and then a "loan" of $36,000 in cash. By the time he got his last gift from Sinclair, Three Rivers Ranch was beginning to look quite prosperous. Fall added another 6,500 acres to the ranch, fixed up the house, put in a new hydroelectric plant, paid off his back taxes, and did some landscaping. The visitor who had been to Three Rivers earlier, when Fall's car kept breaking down on the way from the station to the ranch, returned for another visit, driving his own car this time, and, as he got closer to Three Rivers, he felt increasingly "lost." He knew he was on the right road, he said, "but I couldn't locate myself. And I was puzzled, and I discovered when I came down there that a change had been made in the road going to Mr. Fall's place, was the cause of my confusion. There had been pillars built up to this road, and beautiful woven wire fence put along, and trees planted, and beautiful concrete gutters, and a very expensive road, as far as I could see, up to the ranch house. I couldn't see all the way. The conditions were so changed I couldn't recognize it."

The improvement in Fall's financial condition was nice, but modest compared to that of Doheny and Sinclair. Doheny figured his Elk Hills property was worth $100 million. Sinclair figured his property at Teapot Dome was worth the same. Sinclair found a way to convert some of his holdings into instant cash. He formed the Mammoth Oil Company, with a capital stock of 2,005,000 shares, all of them issued in his own name. He exchanged a portion of these shares for stock in the Hyva Corporation, a family corporation. The Hyva Corporation then traded a portion of these Mammoth Oil shares for 250,000 shares of Sinclair Consolidated Oil, at the same time that it purchased shares of Mammoth Oil at $17 (when the market price was $50 per share). When all these transactions are sorted out, it appears that Sinclair made a profit of $17,059,700 on about one-third of the shares of Mammoth Oil, without somehow ever letting them go.

The Elk Hills and Teapot Dome deals were okay, but they were nothing compared to the idea Harry Sinclair had for an even bigger operation. Soon after Fall had secured the deals with Doheny and Sinclair, he told Harding that he felt he had done about as much as he could in the service of the public and he thought he would like to retire to his ranch. Harding accepted his resignation with regret, and Fall went to Three Rivers.

Fall had only just arrived at Three Rivers when he got the telegram from Harry Sinclair, asking him to come to New York at once, prepared to leave for Europe. Fall telegraphed back for details. It turned out that Sinclair was after a lease on the oil lands in the southern half of the Soviet Union's Sakhalin Island.

Fall would go, he telegraphed to Sinclair, but he was short of cash. Colonel Zevely arranged for $25,000 worth of Liberty Bonds to be dispatched to Fall's bank, along with another $10,000 in cash to Fall for expenses. Sinclair, Fall, and Archibald Roosevelt set off for Moscow. They negotiated an agreement without a hitch, almost overnight, for an awesome amount of Russian oil. They signed the contract and returned to New York at once in the highest of spirits.

There was only one hitch to the agreement. The Russians had made a single stipulation: within five years of the date of the contract, the United States government must recognize the Soviet Union. All Sinclair, Fall, and Archie Roosevelt needed to do was to alter the foreign policy of the United States, and they stood to make hundreds and thousands of millions.

Fall did not lose a moment in starting to work. When his ship docked in New York, the former secretary of the interior was greeted by newspaper reporters. How had he liked Russia? The Soviet Union, Fall declared solemnly to the reporters, was not as bad as it had been painted. In fact, he said, he looked forward to the day that the Soviet Union would be recognized by the United States.

The King of the Bootleggers Returns

SOMEHOW, MRS. MABEL Walker Willebrandt had been appointed assistant attorney general in charge of Prohibition enforcement—perhaps because she had been recommended to Harding by that undependable Progressive Hiram Johnson, and Harding, eager to harmonize things with his opponent for the presidential nomination, let Johnson have this bit of patronage. In any case, it turned out that Mrs. Willebrandt, once given the job, to nearly everyone's consternation, did it.

Born in a sod house in Kansas, she did not attend school until the age of thirteen and then completed all her high school studies in three years. She was expelled from a small college in Parkville, Missouri, because she disagreed with the president over his Calvinist views on predestination. "She couldn't imagine," according to Thomas Coffey, "that she was not the mistress of her own fate." She turned to teaching high school and fell in love with the princi-

George Remus, the king of the bootleggers, wastes none of his charm on the newsman who snuck up on him for this quick snapshot. (United Press International Photo)

pal, Alfred Willebrandt, a frail man. When he decided he needed to move west for the sake of his health, she married him and went with him, to care for him.

She studied law at night, was admitted to the bar, was elected president of the Women Lawyers' Club and of the Women's Professional Club, and was separated from her husband in 1916. "Dressed invariably," Coffey says, "in a blue or grey suit so severely tailored as to obscure her trim athletic figure, she was the first to arrive at her office and the last to leave. She took an ice-cold bath every morning before breakfast, and often she walked to work." She achieved her remarkable self-discipline at a cost: she told no one of her urge to adopt a child, and when at last she did adopt a girl, she kept it a secret from her associates. As for Prohibition, she had always been a moderate drinker herself, but when the prohibition laws were passed, she gave up liquor at once and saw no reason others should not do the same. She felt that the law of the land, good or bad, must be obeyed and enforced.

Shortly after midnight on October 21, 1921, six federal agents moved in on the bottling works at Remus's Death Valley Farm. A few lights were burning in the farmhouse; a few cars were parked nearby. The agents made their way silently up to the house, moved quickly to the front door, opened it, flicked on the lights, and

Mabel Willebrandt, an assistant attorney general of the United States, took it on her own—to the amazement of Washington insiders—to nail Remus.

announced the arrest. Six armed men, dozing or sound asleep, raised their hands in surrender. One man dashed out the back door, but stopped and dropped his gun the moment one of the agents called out to stop. Remus and six of his men were indicted.

In New York, Jess Smith took another payment and assured Remus that he had nothing to worry about. The indictment might lead to a trial. It might even be that a jury would convict Remus. Even so, Remus need not worry. The case would then go to a court of appeals whose verdict could never be reversed.

Nan Pays a Visit

ONE TIME WHEN Nan Britton arrived in Washington to see Harding, Tim Slade told her "how they were 'putting it over' on 'the Chief,' as he often called Mr. Harding." Nan determined to tell the president what Tim had said, and so, as soon as she had been guided through the halls and Cabinet Room into the president's office, she blurted out to Harding, "Sweetheart, Tim Slade says they are doing things behind your back down here to hurt you. . . ."

Harding smiled. "Say, darling, don't you worry about *me!* I'm all right."

She judged from his expression that a look of relief must have passed across her face. She said that she couldn't see what anyone "*could* do to 'double-cross' a *President,*" but she did wish he would be careful.

He was surrounded by friends, Harding told her; no one was putting anything over on him.

Harding was more worried, in fact, about the embarrassment that Nan might cause him, and whenever he gave her a few hundred or five-hundred dollar bills, he would always remind her to be careful about the way she spent it, so that no one would talk. Once when she appeared in a squirrel coat, Harding did say that the coat was beautiful, but he was clearly anxious about it. "Nan, darling," he said, "do be careful! How in the world do you explain these expensive-looking things?"

He was even more vexed when a picture of their daughter, Elizabeth Ann, appeared in the newspaper. Back home, Nan had left Elizabeth Ann in the bathroom for a moment while she went into the bedroom to get something, and Elizabeth Ann, then two-and-a-half years old, had locked herself in the bathroom. Nan called the fire department, and newspaper reporters came along to get the amusing story of a fireman carrying a little girl down the ladder from a bathroom window. When Nan showed the newspaper picture to Harding, who had never seen his daughter, he said, "Oh, Nan, *why* did you allow it? Why *did* you allow it?"

The newspaper reporters did not know whose child it was, of course, but Harding was upset by it anyway. After a few moments, however, he relaxed and took a closer look at the photograph.

"Really, Nan, she's much like you!"

"Oh, darling," said Nan, "she's much more like *you!* Why, just look at her *eyes!*"

"Well," said Harding slowly, not overeager to claim a paternal resemblance, "if she's as sweet a baby as her mother is a woman . . ."

Sometimes Nan would bring along penciled scratches—"letters"—from Elizabeth Ann, which she would show to Harding; and it was at those moments that she usually cried. "I could not talk long with her father about her without crying." She had arranged for Elizabeth Ann to be officially adopted by her sister and brother-in-law, and at times she was overcome by depression at the thought that she could neither acknowledge Harding as her lover, nor Elizabeth Ann as her daughter, nor live in the same town with Harding, nor let Elizabeth Ann know who her father was. At times like these, "Mr. Harding's eyes would grow heavy with sadness as he turned the conversation into other channels and pulled out a ready handkerchief to dry my eyes. He would try so hard to bring a smile to my face!"

She asked Harding if she couldn't come to Washington to get a job, but that never struck Harding as a prudent idea. She was once sitting in Harding's office when his secretary came in with a question about something he had written.

"Can't read it?" said Harding with a smile.

He interpreted the passage for his secretary, as Nan sat thinking how well she knew his handwriting, how easily she could have deciphered the passage. When the secretary left, she said, "Oh, I wish *I* could work for you, darling!"

Harding smiled—"the old smile of indulgence and love I liked to think he smiled best at *me*—but shook his head. 'It will never do, dearie,' he said. Then he went on to picture in the face of his refusal how he would *love to have me,* and how, if I *were* his stenographer he would give me *all* his dictation just to have me with him, and he feared the nation's business would suffer! Thus it was that he would picture for me the things he would love to do, making their impossibility a thing of unspeakable disappointment to me."

From time to time, Harding would try to get Nan a better or a different job elsewhere. He commended her, on one occasion, to the collector of the Port of New York, and the collector evidently tried to find her a job in the Customs House. In fact, Nan had several men in the Customs House trying to find or create a job for her, although they had an embarrassing time of it, since Nan could not do shorthand very well and was not a good typist.

"Don't go off and marry any of the fellows you meet, dearie!" Harding would plead with her, as they sat on the dilapidated couch in the anteroom of his office. "I love you so much, Nan," he would say, blushing slightly and sometimes telling her how it would be once he got out of the burdensome office of the president and returned to Ohio where he would buy a farm, have a lot of farm animals, enjoy the country, and settle down with her and with their daughter, at last—"and I don't like to have you be with anybody else—that's the real truth!"

"And then for a brief space of time—all too brief—we became oblivious to our surroundings, to his identity as President of the United States, and to all the world. 'Why don't you tell me you love me, Nan darling,' he coaxed, and I told him over and over again, as I had told him a thousand times, 'I love you, darling Warren Harding, I love you.' "

XXXI.

The President Remembers His Schoolboy Aspirations

NEWSPAPER EDITORIAL WRITERS were generally impressed by Harding's adminstration in its first year. The *New York Times,* which had at first considered him "the firm and perfect flower of the cowardice and imbecility of the senatorial cabal," had come to conclude that Harding was "gradually assuming undisputed leadership and without offending his former associates in the Senate."

Whether his newspaper clippings went to his head—or some forgotten longing within him commenced to emerge—Harding "deeply wanted," as Herbert Hoover came to notice, "to make a name as President."

After all, as a schoolboy reading his *McGuffey Eclectic Reader,* he had learned the story about George Washington and the cherry tree. Alexander Hamilton had been his hero since earliest boyhood, and was still. He wished, somehow, to rise above himself; but he did not seem to know quite how to do it.

Men who became legendary heroes—Henry Ford at left and Thomas Edison at center—while away some hours with a man who became a president of the United States.

Charlie Forbes, before he had met his comeuppance, had gone to play poker with the president one evening, and after the game broke up, Harding took Forbes aside and strolled with him out onto the White House lawn. Harding was, he told Forbes, dreadfully unhappy: his life had been empty. And then, to Forbes's amazement, the president simply broke down and cried.

XXXII.

Things Begin to Come Apart: Gaston Means Investigates Nan Britton

ACCORDING TO GASTON Means, whose word is always suspect when it is not an outright lie, Mrs. Harding called him in one day. "I entered the White House," he said, "as usual through what I now called the 'viaduct entrance.' The guards within the White House knew me by this time and passed me quietly on to Mrs. Harding's private apartment upstairs."

He found her door slightly ajar when he rapped. Through the door, he saw her standing across the room looking out of a window. In her right hand, he noticed, she was gripping some folds of the lace curtain at the window and that she was unconsciously "crushing the folds."

At the sound of his knock, she turned at once.

"Mr. Means," she said. "Come in."

She closed the door behind him and directed him to a couch, where she sat, too, at the opposite end, with a pillow at her back.

"I'm feeling fine this morning," she told him. "My masseur [*sic*] has just finished her treatment. She tells me that I have the firm flesh of a young girl. See?"

She held up her arm for Means to inspect. "The loose violet-colored chiffon sleeves," Means observed, "fell away in soft folds."

"My arms are smooth and firm and white—aren't they? I am very proud of my arms. And—you have noticed I am sure, that my walk has the same elastic spring that I had as a girl. I am really

proud of my walk. I have kept myself young–and I always intend to."

" 'No one is ever any older than they feel,' was my not very original rejoinder," Means recalled.

"Many public men," Mrs. Harding said hesitantly, "many great men have had their careers utterly ruined–and the lives of all their loved ones totally wrecked–by–indiscretions. They have had to forfeit everything that was dear to them–by an act of weakness."

Means could not disagree.

"Warren Harding," Mrs. Harding said at last, "has had a very ugly affair with a girl named Nan Britton from Marion. It goes back to the actual childhood of this girl. . . . I became suspicious . . when she was but a child. . . . She was a greatly over-developed child and wore extremely short dresses above the knees. It was not considered quite decent. And she was always doing everything on earth that she could–to attract Warren's attention. This over-development tended to attract men–on the streets and together with her unusually short dresses, why she attracted attention of course and not in a very nice way. Why, I have watched men–watch her–even before she was in her early teens. . . ."

Mrs. Harding wanted Means to investigate Nan Britton. The president's wife said she already knew that her husband and Nan were having an affair, but it occurred to Means that she was hoping he could disprove it.

"This girl Nan Britton," said Mrs. Harding suddenly, "has a child and she claims that Warren Harding is the father of it!"

Means was too astonished to speak.

"I don't believe it!" the Duchess said.

Where, Means inquired, would he find Nan Britton?

Gaston B. Means, his pockets full of papers or sandwiches, peers about with the customary sharp eye of the plainclothesman. (United Press International Photo)

"That girl! Oh–everywhere! She stays with this sister in Chicago sometimes–God alone knows where she calls home. But listen! You can find out. I want you to find out and put her under surveillance immediately, day and night."

Would Means accept the assignment?

He would. He would start, he said, with Nan's date of birth.

"Oh–I don't care to know anything about her birth," said Mrs. Harding. "I know all about that. Don't waste time on things like that. . . . Begin at twelve years of age."

Means understood his job perfectly: he was to prove that Nan and Harding were not lovers. Failing that, he was to prove that Nan had many lovers who could have been the father of her child.

XXXIII.

An Incidental Nuisance: The People Rise Up

WARTIME PRICES CONTINUED to go up after the war ended. The cost of food had more than doubled in seven years. And so the years 1919 and 1920 were a time of strikes not only for higher wages, but also strikes for lower prices, buyers' strikes, and renters' strikes. Even William McAdoo, a former secretary of the treasury, joined the buyers' strike, appearing in a pair of trousers with patches on them to show he was making do with old clothes. Wearing old clothes became quite the vogue; old dresses were the fashionable style, and cotton bib overalls came off the farm and into the office now and then. It seemed that everyone was joining one sort of strike or another.

Then prices began to fall, and with the falling prices, businesses failed, mortgages were foreclosed, some employers succeeded in convincing their workers to take wage cuts, others simply let their workers go; and unemployment rose to 11 percent. As inflation gave way to recession, the two forces intermingled, and whipsawed the country, and a general, alarming sense of chaos impressed itself on nearly everyone's imaginations.

In 1919 there had been strikes of harbor workers in New York and of 35,000 dress and shirtwaist makers, a strike of shipbuilders in Seattle, a threatened strike of 86,000 packers, a strike in New York of 30,000 cigar makers, and in Chicago of 30,000 construction workers, of 70,000 railroad shopmen in Chicago, and of streetcar, elevated, and subway workers in Boston and Chicago, of New England railroad shopmen and of Chicago carpenters and steelworkers and of Boston policemen and of New York actors and of bituminous coal miners.

During Harding's administration, the bituminous coal miners went out on strike again, led by John L. Lewis, the son of a Welsh miner and a miner himself, a man with a thick shock of hair and a prize fighter's face, who looked as though he wanted an excuse for a fist fight. The owners demanded that the miners take a pay cut, back to the pay scale of 1917. Lewis declared that the miners would never settle for that, and he called out 600,000 miners.

In Herrin, Illinois, mine owners hired armed strikebreakers to go in and work the mines. The miners had seen bands of strikebreakers before; they had been clubbed and shot by them. At Herrin, union miners closed in with rifles and dynamite. The county sheriff and his men stood aside, and the miners attacked. The strikebreakers, even though they were armed with machine guns, could not withstand the siege. They raised a white flag. The miners accepted their surrender and forced them to run a gauntlet on their way out of the mine: twenty-one of them were lynched, shot, or beaten to death, in what came to be called the Herrin Massacre.

XXXIV.

The People Crushed

HARDING, WHO HAD tried to remain aloof, stepped in at last. He asked Lewis to have the workers return to work, temporarily, on the basis of the current wage scale, and then to promise to agree to the recommendations of a presidential commission that Harding would appoint to determine a fair settlement. The proposal was doubly rigged against the miners: eight of the eleven members of the commission would be owners or Harding-appointed representatives of the "general public" (who could be expected to be opposed to the miners), and in any case, the commission would return to the old method of determining settlements district by district, destroying the national union by dividing it. Lewis declined.

"I want to convey to you in this message," Harding telegraphed to the governors of twenty-eight coal-mining states, "the assurance of the prompt and full support of the federal government whenever and wherever you find your own agencies of law and order inadequate to meet the situation." The president's message was somewhat vague, but the governors—and the miners—all interpreted it the same way: if the owners wanted to reopen their mines, whether with strikebreakers or any other kind of laborers, they would have federal troops to back them. With rumors of a shooting war, all sides pulled back for a brief respite.

In the very midst of the coal strike, the Railroad Labor Board, which had been constituted in 1920 to hear arguments and determine wage and work-rule settlements for railroad workers, ordered a $48 million (13 percent) wage cut for 400,000 maintenance-of-way railroad workers. The board followed this order eight days later with another decision: to cut the pay of 400,000 railroad shopmen by $60 million. Ten days after that the board ordered $26.5 million cut from the payrolls of 325,000 clerks and signalmen. The railroad shopmen walked out.

"The Red agents of the Soviet Government," said Harry Daugherty, "who had bored into the organization of our coal miners . . . worked day and night, by inflammatory circulars and fanatical speakers, to precipitate a clash of arms." Their goal was nothing less than to "tie up every artery of commerce in America," to destroy the "foundations of the Republic," to "overthrow our government and substitute a Soviet Regime." Daugherty knew his duty. He went to the president and told him "that the coal strike would have to be broken, or we must surrender to the gentlemen in Moscow who were directing it."

Daugherty, uninterested in economics or the study of historical phenomena in general, himself a schemer and conniver who always had dozens of small and large plots and conspiracies and counterplots and deals and string pullings going at the same time, could only assume that everyone else did, too, and that, somewhere in the world, there was a great and greatly malevolent, master plotter who was trying to do him in. Whether Harding was entirely convinced by Daugherty seems doubtful, although, once again, he found Daugherty's counterplottings useful.

"I've a war map on the wall of my office," Daugherty told Harding, "in which pins are stuck daily marking the spot where a train has been wrecked, a bridge dynamited, a riot has broken out, a worker been kidnapped, another assaulted, a murder committed. Hundreds of cases are covered up. Men are maimed and killed and the crimes concealed.

"I have records piled high in black and white, from eye-witnesses whose words are beyond question. Of known murders by the strikers. A thousand and five hundred cases of felonious assault with intent to kill. Sixty-five accounts of kidnapping accompanied by brutal assault, eight cases of tar and feathers. . . .

"The real import of this movement is not on the surface. You must look deeper to find it. We are face to face with a determined conspiracy to overturn the government itself."

The Soviets, said Daugherty, planned to seize control of the labor unions first and convert them into "fighting units." These would then be fused into a single whole. The leaders of this conspiracy could be found easily enough: they were leaders of the "Liberal" groups and of the "Civil Liberties," "Parlor Bolshevik," and "Intelligentsia" groups.

"The class struggle," Daugherty continued, "which so long appeared in forms unrecognizable to millions of workers, develops now into open combat, civil war."

"It looks like it, doesn't it?" the president muttered—whether in agreement or fatigue at the harangue is not clear.

"Looks like it!" Daugherty shouted. "It *is* civil war. And it's so widespread and serious we don't dare allow the facts to be known! The Labor Lobby in Washington that attempts a stranglehold on legislation is no longer conservative. It is controlled by the Red borers in its ranks."

Harding had no reply to this.

"We can't afford," Daugherty went on, or claimed he did, lecturing the president right into the carpet, "to proclaim a condition of civil war at this time, though we are actually in it. The reckless young of the rising generation, who have caught the spirit of anarchy from the war conditions, have begun to question all things you and I hold sacred and worthwhile."

"Well," said Harding at last, having suffered Daugherty's full course on The Menace, "what is your answer to this?"

"Direct, drastic, firm action by the United States Government. Can it live and move and assert its power? Have we a government?"

"I believe," Daugherty remembered–or imagined–Harding's reply, "we have."

XXXV. An Absent-Minded Elimination of Free Speech, Assembly, And So Forth

WHATEVER HIS CONVERSATION with Daugherty may have been, Harding did decide to go ahead with a dramatic speech to Congress, where he spoke to a packed joint session of House and Senate. This gave him a superb opportunity to appear decisive, forceful, a firm leader, and altogether presidential.

"We must assert," Harding declared, "the doctrine that in this Republic the first obligation and the first allegiance of every citizen, high and low, is to his government. . . . And to hold that government to be the just and unchallenged sponsor for public welfare and the liberty, security, and rights of all its citizens.

"No matter what clouds may gather, no matter what storms may ensue, no matter what hardships may attend, or what sacrifices may be necessary, government by law must and will be sustained."

Daugherty was dispatched on the night train to Chicago, where he appeared before Judge James Wilkerson, who had been

Harry Daugherty was always one step ahead of the law, especially when he was the attorney general of the United States.

appointed Justice of the Northern Illinois District Court by Harding, on Daugherty's recommendation. Wilkerson issued the injunction that Daugherty had drafted: it affirmed the open shop and the right to work and forbade union members from interfering with strikebreakers' coming in to take over their jobs. More than that, however, it enjoined union members from the exercise of all sorts of their constitutional rights. They were not to be allowed to "loiter" near railroad offices or yards; they were not to "congregate" near railroad shops or terminals; they were not to picket; they were not even to speak to anyone to persuade them not to work; they were not allowed "in letters, circulars, telegrams, telephones, or word of mouth, or through interviews in the papers, [to] encourage or direct anyone to leave or enter the service of the railroad companies."

The injunction stunned the strikers and broke the strike within forty-eight hours. The mine workers, already chilled by Harding's apparent promise to call out federal troops, found their way back to the negotiating table, too, and agreed to a settlement worked out by a friend of Andrew Mellon's–the "Cleveland formula," similar to Harding's old proposal.

When Daugherty returned triumphantly to Washington, he discovered that his injunction had stunned his fellow cabinet members, too. None of the members of the cabinet objected to the intention or the outcome of the injunction, not Hoover or Hughes or Mellon or Davis or any of the others, but almost all of them were appalled at its heavy-handedness.

Hughes and Hoover went on record that the injunction was "outrageous in law as well as morals." Hoover pointed out to Daugherty that the injunction was a mistake because it virtually eliminated civil liberties. Theodore Roosevelt, Jr., who had been made an assistant secretary of the navy and was sitting in for the absent Denby, pointed out that the injunction was too broad and that, furthermore, it was politically imprudent–because congressional elections were coming up, an observation that gave pause to all the men sitting around the table.

Harding turned to Daugherty and told him to withdraw those parts of the injunction that infringed on civil liberties.

Daugherty left the cabinet meeting with his feelings badly bruised. Far from getting the congratulations, indeed the adulation, he thought he deserved for having saved the Republic, he had been roundly abused. At that moment, Daugherty understood, a Communist conspiracy was out to get him.

XXXVI.

A Little of the Old Soft Soap

POLITICS IS COMPOSED almost as much of symbolic acts, or appearances, as it is of actual policies. Sometimes a symbolic act will prepare the public for the policy to follow; sometimes the symbolic act will announce the beginning of the policy; sometimes it will boost a policy along. Often, however, a symbolic act is most useful when it flatly contradicts an actual policy–helping to confuse and draw the sting from the opposition. To speak one way and act another will allow a politician to stand on both sides of an issue.

Eugene V. Debs, the grand old man of American socialism, had been sent to the Atlanta penitentiary in 1918 for "actively and purposely" obstructing the draft. While he was in jail, he had been nominated, as he had so often been in the past, to run for president in 1920 on the Socialist ticket–and he had gotten almost a million votes.

Although Debs was understood, first, to be a Socialist and an antiwar critic of the government, he had come, also, to be regarded more generally as a champion of outsiders of other sorts. "An after-effect of the Great War," said Mark Sullivan, "had been irritation on the part of some labor groups which, fostered by a few radical leaders, seemed pointed towards serious social unrest. These leaders were making skillful use of Debs's incarceration. Debs, they declared, was the victim of persecution by the same profit-greedy men who had maneuvered America into the war and made labor do the fighting while they amassed riches." Debs became, in spite of himself, the hero of the left, and of labor.

When Harding took office, he was besieged with letters and petitions seeking Debs's release from jail. Another of America's Socialist leaders, Norman Thomas, who had worked for a time as a newsboy for Harding's Marion newspaper, wrote to Harding to urge the release of all "political" prisoners, as Woodrow Wilson had dubbed them, of whom there were three classes: those who had personally tried to avoid the draft, for whatever reason; those who had spoken out against the war as a matter of principle; and those who, such as members of the International Workers of the World, advocated the overthrow of the wartime government.

Of all those jailed during the war, 13,735 had already been released. Only several hundred, including Debs, remained in jail. In Britain, Italy, and Belgium, all such prisoners had long since been released. Only the United States still held such "political" prisoners. Although the American Legion opposed the pardoning of any of these prisoners, the World War Veterans favored a general amnesty. It was pointed out that of all the seventy-six Wobblies in jail, none had actually committed a violent act. "They had received a total of eight hundred years of jail time," as Andrew Sinclair has written, "for *speaking* against the government and the war." George Bernard Shaw joined the chorus for their release, along with H. G. Wells, Upton Sinclair, and Henri Barbusse. Still, Harding waited, letting the pressure build even more.

In Daugherty's view, none of the prisoners ought ever to be released. The crimes of the Wobblies, said Daugherty, "were more

Eugene V. Debs, socialist firebrand and revolutionary, could be as presentable as a Presbyterian usher on Sunday.

horrible than outright murder." If any of them had to be pardoned, then they ought to be made to take a loyalty oath in which they acknowledged their crime, expressed contrition, and promised to behave themselves in the future. Daugherty said, however, that Debs should not take such an oath. "He is such an habitual violator of the laws of this country and has such a chronic disregard for his country and is so ignorant of his obligation to society that he might go upon his honor, if he has any."

Harding instructed Daugherty to bring Debs up from Atlanta and have a chat with him—perhaps to see whether he still seemed like a dangerous man. Debs was put on a train, without escort, and sent up to Daugherty's office. Jess Smith met him at Union Station and drove him over to see Daugherty. Debs and the attorney general sat and talked all day. Daugherty had to duck out for a lunch date (Debs asked to have some fresh fruit brought in for him), but he returned after lunch and talked through the afternoon. He found Debs a straightforward man—"woefully wrong," but "sincere, gentle, and tender. . . . He unfolded frankly his ideas on government, his ideas on religion, his own case, the cause of Socialism with which he was identified, his beliefs and disbeliefs. A more eloquent and fascinating recital I never heard fall from the lips of any man. . . . I found him a charming personality, with a deep love for his fellow man. . . . He did not flinch at anything. He looked every fact squarely in the face. He made no apologies. . . ." Daugherty always admired a man who did not apologize for himself, and so he eased up on his opposition to a pardon for Debs. Jess took Debs back to the train station, and along the way as they got to talking about prison life, Debs mentioned that one thing he particularly missed was toothpicks. Jess stopped the car, dashed into a store, and brought out a big bundle of quill toothpicks to the grateful Debs.

At last, when the campaign for Debs had reached its peak, Harding told Daugherty that he was going to pardon Debs. Daugherty, overcoming his distaste for the proposal, suggested the end of the year, 1921. Harding said no, he wanted to release Debs on Christmas Eve so that Debs could spend Christmas Day with his wife. Daugherty said such an act would desecrate Christmas. Nonetheless, Harding released Debs on Christmas Eve, 1921, and asked him to come up to Washington and stop by the White House the day after Christmas.

When Debs appeared at the door of Harding's office, the president bounced out of his chair. "Well," Harding said happily, "I have heard so damned much about you, Mr. Debs, that I am now very glad to meet you personally." Harding, like Daugherty, always found that he had some sympathy for the outsider, if he could put aside other considerations for a moment. Debs and Harding had a jolly conversation, and Debs, on his way out, told reporters that "Mr. Harding appears to me to be a kind gentleman, one whom I believe possesses humane impulses."

Harding, standing up for Debs—and against six hundred thousand miners, four hundred thousand railroad shopmen, and millions of other workers, farmers, renters, and buyers—came out slightly better than even.

XXXVII.

What Gaston Means Found Out

MEANS SENT SEVERAL men at once to Marion, and working from grammar school up, they soon discovered two young women who had gone all through school with Nan. "These girls knew little or nothing at first hand of Nan Britton. They said—she was a prude, a stick, a frost. That she didn't care for boys."

From the young women, the detectives learned of several boys who had had "crushes" on Nan. The boys—by this time young men—"separately and candidly stated that Nan Britton never allowed any boy to take privileges."

Everyone in Marion recalled Nan as a "good and virtuous girl," who might have kissed a boy—or, to be precise, allowed a boy to kiss her—but that was all. The investigators followed Nan's journey out into the world, interviewed her former landladies, found out what her expenses had been, what she had paid for room and board, where she had bought her clothes and what she had paid for them, where she had worked and what her salary had been, what she had earned and what she had spent, "almost to the penny."

Means's men learned that Nan was a "very careful and prudent young woman." Her laundry bills were small–she did her own washing much of the time. She made sure her shoes were mended and did not splurge on shoes and clothes. She bought "only the barest necessities."

The detectives learned that Nan was vivacious and popular, "but cared nothing for men." Many young men had sought her–all in vain. "One landlady reported that she had but one picture of a man in her room and that one picture was always on her dresser. We made a quick deduction."

In short, Means concluded, "Nan Britton had no lover *but* Mr. Harding." She lived modestly, did her own laundry, had a winter coat dyed to save money, bought sparingly, paid her bills, and had "the respect and admiration of everybody who knew her." She was entirely faithful to Harding; it may even be that she loved him.

This news was dreadful enough; but, what was worse, Means had managed to get into Nan's apartment in Chicago, and he had brought back some letters that Harding had written to Nan.

When Means told Mrs. Harding about the letters, "she gazed at me in amazement. . . . Her frozen countenance for the moment forgot its mask of immobility. The muscles and nerves of her face worked. She swallowed hard once or twice." She could not speak.

At last, when she asked to see them, Means said he could not show them to her. She had asked only for information, not for stolen goods. He would keep them.

"Are you a machine–or a human being? Have you no heart in you? Don't you know I've got to have and see those letters?"

Means resisted. Mrs. Harding walked up and down the room, her Spanish shawl, having slipped from her shoulders, dragging behind her on the floor. She insisted on seeing the letters. Means resisted still.

"Go get me those letters," she screamed at him." I want to see those letters with my own eyes."

In the end, of course, he gave them to her–forty-page and sixty-page letters, all tied together just as he had found them, "the same pink silk corset ribbon, the same knots–and all arranged in chronological order."

Mrs. Harding grabbed one of the letters at random from the bundle as she asked Means to tell her just how and where he had found them. Means replied as she began to look at the first letter, but she heard nothing he said. Nor was she reading the letter she had taken from its envelope. She had glanced at it only and put it aside and had taken another and then another until all the letters were scattered on the table. She went on taking the letters from the envelopes, glancing at them frantically, taking up still another bundle and scattering it on the table. Her face, said Means, was as "white as chalk" and her hands "were like transparent wax."

He decided to slip out and leave her with the letters, and as he went out of the room, he could hear her saying, "Could you believe it. . . . Oh–oh! . . ."

No Escape

"WARREN HARDING," THE Duchess declared another day to Gaston Means, having thought of a new way to escape the news that Means had brought her, "is not capable of having a child, therefore he is not the father of Nan Britton's child."

"If sure of your premise," said the old deducer.

"We have had no children. I have demonstrated my ability. I've had a living son by a former marriage. . . . The thing I want you to do—is to prove for me that Warren Harding cannot be the father of a child."

Once again, Means's men hit the road. Harding had been so often troubled by his chronic indigestion that he had consulted a string of doctors. Evidently, he, too, had wondered whether he was capable of having a child: at least several of the doctors had examined him with a view to settling these doubts. Means acquired documents from a physician's office in Columbus, Ohio, and from

Johns Hopkins University in Baltimore. In the Johns Hopkins documents, "the chemical and microscopic tests were designated by a number." Both tests indicated that Harding could father a child.

When Means broke the news to Mrs. Harding, she was adamant. "I don't care," she said, "if a million eminent specialists said he could be a father–I know it is not true."

Means could not think what to say.

"Wait!" said Mrs. Harding. "All I want now to confirm my own proof is a good look into the face of that child. . . . Your next assignment from me is this: bring that child here for me to see!"

"Mrs. Harding . . . you want to turn me into a kidnapper."

Her face, said Means, "her face flamed. She was furious."

"You won't do that?"

"No. I won't."

The King of the Bootleggers Cashes in His Chips

REMUS WENT ON trial in the U.S. District Court in Cincinnati, flanked by six attorneys and thirteen of his employees who had been named as codefendants. He was confident and smiling. No one had been caught selling any liquor at the farm: on other matters, he was covered by permits and the provisions of the law.

Unfortunately, on the first day of the trial, a sworn statement was introduced saying that at least one man had bought a case of whiskey at the farm. The next day, the wife of one of Remus's night watchmen testified that trucks came and went all the time transporting whiskey. On the third day, the government produced a string of witnesses who said they had bought whiskey at the farm. Remus was sentenced to two years at the federal penitentiary at Atlanta.

"We will, of course, file our appeal," said Remus, "and I hope for better results if we can obtain a new trial." Within a few days,

Remus was in Washington to see Jess Smith, and Remus was beginning to lose his patience. Had he known he was going to lose the case, he said, he would have pleaded guilty himself, taken all the blame, and made sure his thirteen employees did not have to go to jail.

Smith was unperturbed. The court of appeals would surely reverse the verdict. If not, then a commutation of sentence would be forthcoming or a reversal in the Supreme Court. Remus had nothing to worry about. Jess had it on the authority of the attorney general that neither Remus nor any of his associates would ever be sent away to Atlanta.

Remus put aside his worries, and to welcome in 1923, Remus invited a hundred couples to a New Year's Eve party. By this time, Remus's estate had been handsomely landscaped; the home had been furnished with antiques; the walls were hung with early American paintings; the swimming pool alone had cost more than $100,000. Small dining tables had been placed around the pool, which had been built to resemble a Roman bath, and flowers and plants decorated the room; young women in white tights served champagne, Bourbon, and gin, and an orchestra played at one end of the pool, while a professional troupe from Chicago performed a water ballet. Imogene herself appeared at one moment in a revealing one-piece suit, and dove into the water to the applause of the guests.

Remus himself, because he did not drink, slipped away from the party in the middle of the night and retired to his library with a dish of ice cream to read for a while. As dawn approached, he emerged again, in time for the giving of party favors. The young women in white tights brought a small gift to each of the male guests—a box containing a diamond tiepin or diamond cuff links, or some similar bit of jewelry.

Then, as the party was breaking up and it was time for the guests to leave, they went to the front door—and there they saw the presents that Remus had in mind for the women. Up the long driveway, in the dawn light, came a grand stream of fifty brand-new

1923 Pontiacs, one for each woman, as a gesture of Remus's friendship.

Shortly thereafter, Remus's case came up on appeal. The court of appeals upheld the verdict of the lower court. Remus was sentenced to serve two years and six months in the Atlanta penitentiary. It could not be fixed. He went to jail. He had paid Jess Smith $500,000—or perhaps twice that amount—for nothing.

XL.

Things Get Out Of Hand

Samuel Gompers, the head of the American Federation of Labor, formerly a cigarmaker, a jovial fellow, an Elk and a Mason, a profoundly conservative man who believed unions should stick to bargaining for wages and stay out of radical politics, was finally moved to attack the Harding administration.

Gompers, an immigrant who had studied the U.S. Constitution in order to become a citizen, understood the difference between Jess Smith and Harry Daugherty. Smith, with his deals for liquor and fight films and kickbacks, was corrupt. But Daugherty, with his injunction, was a threat to the Constitution itself. To steal money was lousy and unfair. But to steal power was to threaten the very Republic that safeguarded every citizen's freedom. It is one thing to skirt the rules; it is another thing to eliminate them. Jess was involved in some lowdown, dirty politics. Harry was involved in high crimes and misdemeanors.

Samuel Gompers, a funny little flag-waving reactionary immigrant, knew his Constitution and helped to preserve it.

Gompers sent Jackson Ralston, the lawyer for the American Federation of Labor, over to see Congressman Oscar Keller of Minnesota. Keller, a nervous, high-strung man was, unfortunately, not the strongest ally Gompers could find—"an absurd creature," Samuel Hopkins Adams called him, "who might have been imagined by Gilbert and set to music by Sullivan." But he was suggestible. With Jackson Ralston's coaching, Keller introduced a resolution in the House, impeaching the attorney general for "abridging freedom of speech, freedom of the press, the right of the people peaceably to assemble," and a number of other crimes against the Constitution.

Keller had not taken the time to assemble any evidence for his charges, but he had heard a great many rumors, and he found some colleagues who were eager to join with him. The farm bloc, happy to damage the Harding administration, joined in calling for hearings before the judiciary committee. Other representatives, some who had friends or contributors who insisted that Daugherty was prosecuting antitrust cases selectively, joined the move for impeachment. Still other representatives had heard stories that the Justice Department prosecuted war profiteers selectively, or sold pardons to criminals, or even that Daugherty had put Bureau of Investigation agents up to spying on members of Congress with a view to blackmailing or intimidating them.

"Let an individual," said Samuel Hopkins Adams, "or a constituted body, such as an investigating committee, attempt to clean up or pry into evil conditions, and the Bureau set in movement its formidable machinery of espionage, menace, and oppression."

The rumor was that agents of the bureau were breaking into offices, tapping telephones, copying private correspondence. No one was safe. The executive branch of government was trying to subdue the legislative branch. Fear for the Constitution, and fear for the individual skins of congressmen, coalesced. It was just the sort of opportunity that members of Congress love.

"Well, let me ask you," as Senator Wheeler put it to Gaston Means in a later investigation of the attorney general's operations, "at whose direction did you investigate Senator Caraway?"

MR. MEANS: "I investigated him through Mr. Jess Smith's direction."

SENATOR WHEELER: "You investigated him through Mr. Jess Smith's direction?"

MR. MEANS: "Yes. . . ."

SENATOR WHEELER: "Was that at the time that Mr. Caraway was making some attacks in the Senate on Attorney General Daugherty?"

MR. MEANS: "No. He had made some attacks on President Harding, too, prior to that, and he had made attacks on the Attorney General, too."

SENATOR WHEELER: "Now, Mr. Means, you also investigated Senator La Follette, did you not?"

MR. MEANS: "Yes."

SENATOR WHEELER: "And you went through his offices here, did you not, in the Capitol?"

MR. MEANS: "No; I did not."

SENATOR WHEELER: "You had somebody do it?"

MR. MEANS: "I saw that it was done."

SENATOR ASHURST: "You did what?"

MR. MEANS: "Well, I saw that it was done."

SENATOR ASHURST: "Well, you saw that Senator Caraway's office was gone through?"

MR. MEANS: "No, sir; I did not."

SENATOR ASHURST: "Who did?"

MR. MEANS: "We didn't go through Caraway that way at all, Senator."

SENATOR WHEELER: "You have never gone through my offices yet, have you?"

MR. MEANS: "If somebody will assign me to it, I will do it, though."

SENATOR WHEELER: "Senator Moses suggests to me that I can save time by asking you what senators you have not investigated."

MR. MEANS: "Oh, there are lots of them I haven't. They are a pretty clean body. You don't find much on them, either. You don't find very much."

SENATOR WHEELER: "Now, Mr. Means, coming back to Senator La Follette, you investigated him at the instance of whom?"

MR. MEANS: ". . . I got those [orders] from Mr. Jess Smith. . . . I didn't–investigation with me is–the man is a number; I never ask who he is. It doesn't make any difference. I would just as soon investigate a tramp as anybody else. It doesn't make any difference to me. I never ask who he is or what position he occupies. I designate the number and go ahead and get the facts if I can, and I get nothing but the facts, and report what I find."

SENATOR ASHURST: "Nobody has asserted or supposed anything to the contrary."

MR. MEANS: "I mean by that it doesn't mean anything about investigating a senator. Thousands of people have been investigated. Bishops have been investigated without knowing it. And clergymen."

THE CHAIRMAN: "When did this terrific spy system start in the United States; by what official authority, if you know?"

MR. MEANS: "I have been investigating since I was twenty-one. . . ."

Nonetheless, the Keller investigation got nowhere. The House Judiciary Committee, overwhelmed by rumors, insisted that Keller back up his charges with some facts, something that would definitely, unmistakably tie in Attorney General Daugherty with some specific act. Keller had nothing on Daugherty himself. The committee demanded that Keller appear and testify. Keller held back. The committee then issued a subpoena and told the sergeant at arms to go out into the hall, where Keller was consulting feverishly with Jackson Ralston, and bring Keller in under arrest.

"On hearing the call of the sergeant at arms," Daugherty recalled with pleasure, "Mr. Keller dashed down the corridor and ran at breakneck speed. The ancients believed that the bowels were the seat of the human soul. In this mad flight, the radical leader gave positive proofs of the truth of this faith. Scrubwomen were called at an unusual hour."

Daugherty had squeaked by once again; he was nothing if not fast on his feet. The talk in Washington was that there were a lot of other scandals in the administration that might be exposed at any minute—more gossip about Fall and Forbes and Jess Smith—but it looked as though those stories could be contained, too, until people just forgot them.

XLI.

Things Get More Out Of Hand: Mr. and Mrs. Harding

ACCORDING TO THAT liar Gaston Means, Mrs. Harding confronted Mr. Harding with the goods on Nan in her rooms at the White House. As Means approached the door, he found it once again conveniently open and heard loud voices coming from the room. Through the open door he saw the president stride across the room and leave by another door.

When Means entered, he found Mrs. Harding, "in her inevitable flowered dress, with pale, set face, and determination written all over her countenance . . . like a General on the field of battle . . . her hands hanging straight at her side were clenched until the knuckles were white. She was trembling all over."

"I've had a word with Warren," she said. "He knows now that I know—everything. I have the whip hand."

Suddenly Harding returned to the room. "At a bound, it seemed," he was standing directly in front of Means, "with extended arm, and pointing his finger straight at me. His infuriated face was crimson: he was trembling all over."

"I've instructed the Department of Justice," Harding told Means, "to discharge you. By what authority have you put the President of the United States under surveillance?"

"You ask two questions in one," Means likes to think he told the president confidently. "Which do you want me to answer first?"

Mrs. Harding was still standing where she had been when Means entered. "She kept her composure," Means recalled. "Her thin lips were pressed together."

"Either you prefer," Harding said.

"In reply to your second question, I didn't have you under surveillance–but I did have your mistress and the mother of your child under surveillance."

Harding "staggered back a step or two," Means recalled, "but caught himself by holding to the side of a couch. A small end-table overturned. Mrs. Harding darted behind him, picked up the table and carefully set it upright again."

"Calm yourself, Warren," she said, "now calm yourself. Don't make a scene."

"Well," said Harding to Means, "you'll find that you have been summarily discharged–and your discharge paper is now at your home. . . ."

"Will you," Means replied coolly, "allow me to confirm that statement by using the phone?"

Means phoned home to confirm that he had been fired. When he put down the telephone, Harding turned on him again. Mrs. Harding had apparently told him that Means had got hold of all Nan's letters and diaries.

"Well," said Harding, "what I want you to get down to and get down to right now–is this: where are those papers and letters and documents and articles–all those things that you got for Mrs. Harding. She tells me that you have them."

"She's your wife. What she tells you, you wouldn't question, would you?"

Mrs. Harding had sat down in a low, old-fashioned rocker, and "was rocking violently back and forth." The president had been striding back and forth across the room, his voice choking "with rage and chagrin." Means remembers himself as calm to the point of being sadistic. At last, Harding, seeing that he would not get the letters or diaries from Means, turned to leave the room, and then turned back again at the door and shook his fist at Mrs. Harding.

"You have ruined me," he said. "You have ruined me! You and your contemptible detectives."

Then he turned to Means: "And as for you, you have been discharged and you'll be indicted in twenty-four hours. You will never again put your foot in the White House. And–I'll have those papers. I'll have search warrants–and you'll be under surveillance for the rest of your life."

Means said nothing. He was struck, however, by the fact that the president had "pointed his *finger* at me, but oh, how he did shake his *fist* at Mrs. Harding."

Means was not present for the ensuing scene between the Hardings, but he said that Mrs. Harding told him about it. Mrs. Harding asked the president, finally, "What will you do with me?"

"You can do," Means said Mrs. Harding said the president said, "what you damn please–"

"Warren–Warren–think of our young love–"

"Young love," he said, "our young love! *Love!* I never loved *you.* You want the truth. Now you've got the truth. Young love! You ran me down! God in heaven–young love–you ran me down–"

"Those," said Mrs. Harding, "are the very words that President Harding said to me. The very words–to me, his wife–for thirty-three years. Oh–it was a terrible scene."

Things Get Completely Out Of Hand: Jess Smith

TOWARD THE END, Roxy said, Jess was afraid. He was aware that any number of mistakes might come back to haunt him. When he would take Roxy to the Hotel Deschler for lunch or dinner, he might suddenly say to Roxy, "See that man over there? How does he look to you?"

"Oh," Roxy would say, "he is all right."

"I don't like his looks," Jess would say.

"Don't look at him," Roxy would reply. "He is all right. He is just a traveling man."

Or they would be sitting in the lobby of the hotel in a couple of chairs, and Jess would say, "Don't let us sit here, let us sit over there; let us go over." And they would move to a couch with their backs against the wall.

He had quit drinking. He had never been a heavy drinker, but his whiskey deals had come to worry him so much that he had sworn off drink altogether.

The last time he went home to Ohio, he met Roxy in Columbus and took her at once to the Hotel Deschler, where, as soon as they got into the hotel lobby, he threw his arms around her and said, "I never was so glad to see anyone in my life."

He had wired ahead to tell Roxy to make whatever plans she wanted for Saturday night, but he had apparently forgotten that, for he asked, "What do you want to do?"

She had made plans to go to a dinner dance.

"Let's go home," he said.

"But I've made plans for dinner tonight out at the club."

"Oh."

"You told me to."

"I know. Well, will you do me a favor?"

"What is it?"

"Will you come on home?"

"Why, certainly."

"Let's go home before dark."

He thought they might take an afternoon train down to Washington Court House, and they caught the two o'clock train. Jess had brought along a brief case that seemed to make him nervous. He asked Roxy to carry it.

In the coach, Roxy rode facing forward, Jess faced backward, and Roxy noticed a man, apparently asleep, leaning somewhat over the side of his seat. She was "jabbering away," she remembered, about what changes she planned in the house, and Jess interrupted her.

"Don't talk too loud," Jess said. "He will hear you."

"No," Roxy said. "I'm not saying anything; I'm not saying anything of consequence."

"I don't like the looks of that fellow."

"Oh, stop looking at him."

"I don't like the looks of that fellow."

"Yes; but stop looking at him."

When they reached Washington Court House, Roxy noticed that Jess kept looking behind them.

"Don't do that," she said. "Stop that."

"Well," Jess said, "I wanted to see if that fellow got off the train."

"Don't you do that again."

"All right," he said and smiled and looked a little bit reassured.

But later on, when they were at home, Jess said, in the midst of a conversation, "You have some letters." Roxy was laughing. "I am afraid," Jess told her.

"Of what," she asked him.

"They are going to get me."

She was too unsettled to ask him what he meant, and, later, when she did ask, all he said was that "they passed it to me." She thought he meant that "they" were going to pin the blame on him, for all that "they" had been doing.

"Tell me all about it, Jess. I know so much."

"No," he said, "just cheer me up."

And then, after a while, he said, "Do you miss me when I'm gone?"

One afternoon, when Jess was spending some time out at the Deer Creek shack with Harry Daugherty, who had returned to Washington Court House, too, for a visit, Daugherty was taking a nap when a man from Columbus came to the shack to see him. Jess told the man that Daugherty was napping and could not be disturbed, but the man insisted that it was urgent, and so Jess woke Harry up.

"You know I won't be disturbed," Daugherty shouted at Jess and flew into a temper tantrum. (The caller from Columbus discreetly got out of the shack and drove away.) Daugherty got out of bed, abusing Jess as he dressed, called for his driver to get the car ready, and stormed out of the shack. He meant to leave Jess behind, without a car. Jess called up Mal Daugherty and asked to have a car sent out to the shack, but Mal said he couldn't send anyone until after the bank closed at three o'clock. Finally Harry relented and gave Jess a ride back into Washington Court House, traveling in silence, enraged.

Whether Daugherty had told Jess while they were at the shack that Harding had told Daugherty to send Jess back to Ohio, permanently–because Harding had heard too many rumors about Jess–or whether Daugherty had told Jess even before they got to the shack is unknowable. But the men had clearly reached the breaking point.

When Daugherty dropped Jess off in town, Jess went directly to the hardware store, and although it was well known that Jess had been too frightened all his life even to touch a gun, he bought a pistol, saying to the clerk, "This is for the attorney general."

When Roxy saw him that afternoon, he was holding his head up and seemed to be relieved of a burden, to be in higher spirits than she had seen him in some time. She asked him if things were "all right now."

"Yes," he said. "They are all right now."

The next night, Jess and Daugherty returned to Washington. Apparently Jess was returning to pack his things to take back to Washington Court House. They had, by this time, moved out of Ned McLean's house on H Street to a suite of rooms in the Wardman Park Hotel–but Jess went to the hotel alone. Daugherty went to spend the night in the White House. But Daugherty asked his secretary, a man named Warren Martin, to stay with Jess at the hotel because, said Daugherty, he was worried about Jess.

Early the next morning, Martin told the police, he heard a crash. He thought "it was a door slamming," as Mark Sullivan wrote, "or that a waiter had dropped a tray; but he could not get to sleep again and he went into the sitting-room. Looking into the other bedroom, he saw Jess Smith slumped on the floor, his head in an iron waste-basket and a revolver in his right hand."

"The bullet," said Daugherty, who went to the apartment

shortly after William Burns of the Bureau of Investigation had arrived on the scene, "had driven through his right temple and lodged in the door jamb."

"To my surprise," Daugherty continued, "I found . . . that Jess had destroyed all my house accounts and my personal correspondence. In fact there was hardly anything left pertaining to my personal affairs." All Jess's papers, too, had been destroyed.

Roxy suspected murder, but the case was pooh-poohed and closed at once, never to be reopened.

That night, "as usual," Sullivan wrote, "Daugherty–still a guest of the White House–dined with the Hardings." Mrs. Harding had invited a couple of friends to have dinner with them, to relieve the gloom. Far from being able to cheer up Harding and Daugherty, the guests "were suffused with the numb despair of the hosts," Sullivan wrote. "At the dinner table, only fragmentary sentences were spoken.

"Afterward, a private showing of a motion-picture in the upstairs hall furnished no real diversion–but did happily provide a darkness to five harassed souls, a darkness that saved each countenance from sight of the others. No one spoke. Only from one person came any sound; from time to time Daugherty uttered a long-drawn-out 'O-o-o-o-o-o-o.' "

XLIII.

The President Aspires To Surpass Himself

DAVID LAWRENCE, WHO was then writing a syndicated newspaper column, was the first to break the news that the president had sworn off alcohol. Previously there had been suggestions off the record of presidential abstemiousness; but Lawrence's story had the authority of an official announcement: Harding had quit drinking.

He seemed, at last, to be trying, as Hoover thought he wished to do, to rise above himself. "Something new," said Samuel Hopkins Adams, "was stirring in him." He was no longer tolerating his old political cronies. "Office seekers," said the down-home political commentator "Uncle Henry," in *Collier's* magazine, "wear nose guards and shin protectors when they go to the White House nowadays, an' even then they come out bruised to the color of a California plum."

The patronage dispensers were being given short shrift. Rumors circulated in Washington that Daugherty would resign at any moment. Opposition from the Old Guard senators and the bosses was no longer being tolerated by the White House. Harding even went so far—over the objections of Nan's former employer, Judge Gary of U.S. Steel—as to declare that the twelve-hour workday was a relic of the past and must be ended.

Doubtless Harding was looking forward to the election of 1924, and some of his restless stirring was nothing but electioneering. Yet, everyone sensed a new purposiveness about the president, a renewed wish to be truly presidential. Whether it was "something new" that stirred in him, as Adams thought, or something as old as an Ohio schoolboy's reverence for the office of the presidency, none of the Washington insiders failed to notice the change.

Early in the spring of 1923, Harding decided to move out into the country, to get out of Washington and take a trip through the Middle West and West and on up into Alaska, to try to gather a constituency for a fresh start. He had no great new slogan for himself, but he did his best to come up with something; he decided to call his trip a "Voyage of Understanding."

He departed on June 20, with the Duchess and twenty-two newspaper reporters, five photographers, ten Secret Service men, Doc Sawyer, his secretary George Christian, and other friends and aides. As they moved across the country—stopping now and again in small towns for Harding to stand out on the platform in the sun to make a short speech—he played bridge, talked, and moved restlessly from one side of the car to the other to look out the windows at the passing countryside. He was almost never alone, almost never still.

He had determined to aspire to statesmanship, to redeem himself by casting his presidency suddenly above the sordidness of the politics of the Ohio Gang to some grander plane. But by this time, he was so out of practice at aspiring, his imagination had been so little used in such terms, that he could not think of anything too wonderful.

He chose to speak in favor of a World Court—as though he

would invent the very context in which he himself would be judged good. The World Court was, by this time, a safely popular issue. It was an issue that could attract the old League of Nations crowd—and, at the same time, bring in a lot of others who despised the league but loved the notion of standing for something noble in the world community. The World Court would be something the country could join without being bound in any real way by any international accords. Four out of five voters favored a world court.

Harding had hardly taken a courageous position. He thought he had: his support for the World Court put him in direct opposition to those fearsome old Republican warhorses in the Senate. But Harding had had so little practice in courage that he gave himself more credit than he deserved in standing up for the World Court.

He chose to speak out first in St. Louis—and that, too, was something that must have seemed courageous to him, since St. Louis was the very bastion of isolationism in America.

"I shall not restrict my appeal to your reason," Harding said. "I shall call upon your patriotism. I shall beseech your humanity. I shall invoke your Christianity."

He believed in his cause: he had come at this late date to an issue that perfectly mixed opportunism and idealism, bravery and expediency, vote getting and nobility; it was so wonderful an issue that it might have made him weep.

"I shall reach to the very depths of your love for your fellow countrymen of whatever race or creed throughout the world. . . . My soul yearns for peace. My heart is anguished by the sufferings of war. My spirit is eager to serve. My passion is for justice over force. My hope is in the great court. My mind is made up. My resolution is fixed."

He had meant, before he left on his tour, to speak of the World Court only once or twice. But, as the tour went on, he returned to the subject again and again, expanding on it. As time went on, he discovered that, no matter what the topic of his speech was supposed to be, he almost always worked his way back around to the World Court. He believed in it–and it seemed a relief to him to be able to pour out his heart about something in which he believed.

Doc Sawyer worried about the president. Harding spoke too often, and although the Middle West was languishing in a heat wave, Harding insisted on getting out at every whistle stop for a speech–until his lips had become blistered by the sun, and Doc Sawyer had to apply ice compresses.

Harding worked and reworked his speeches with his own hand, polishing the text so that he was saying just what he wanted. By the time he reached Kansas City, William Allen White noticed that "his lips were swollen and blue, his eyes puffed, and his hands seemed stiff when I shook hands with him." Still, he would not slow down.

In Salt Lake City, he spoke in the auditorium of the Mormon Tabernacle. He was scheduled to speak on the subject of taxation, but he set his text aside at one point. "I am seeking," he said, "American sentiment in favor of an international court of justice. I want America to play her part in helping to abolish war. I want America to have something of a spiritual ideal."

Doc Sawyer became more worried the farther they traveled. By the time the train had reached the Far West, Harding's manner of speaking had become not merely sad but somehow heavy. He was unable to bring himself to make many gestural flourishes. He seemed greatly burdened. By the time they had reached Yellowstone Canyon, Sawyer had told the president that he must not climb any long flights of stairs. The doctor was worried about Harding's heart.

Herbert Hoover joined the presidential party in Tacoma, Washington, to go along on the thousand-mile voyage up into Alaska. The president's entourage all went aboard the ship with happy thoughts of shuffleboard and relaxation, and, indeed, there were movies every night; the navy band held concerts three times a day; there was group singing; there was shuffleboard on the deck. Harding, however, seemed little interested in all these activities. He wanted, rather–compulsively–to play cards. For Hoover, the voyage was dreadful. "As soon as we were aboard ship," Hoover recalled, Harding "insisted on playing bridge, beginning every day immediately after breakfast and continuing except for mealtime often until after midnight. There were only four other bridge players in the party, and we soon set up shifts so that one at a time had some relief."

Harding "played late and slept ill," Samuel Hopkins Adams said. "In his devitalized state he wanted and doubtless needed a drink. But now–conclusive evidence of his fidelity to his new principles–there was nothing available. The presidential luggage carried no liquor." The president was preoccupied, exhausted, unable to rest, and driven. Still he spoke, and continued to speak, of the World Court, and of his hope that his administration would go down in history as a "period of understanding."

XLIV.

The Past Catches Up

JUST AFTER THE ship had reached its northernmost point and turned, as it started to make its way back south, down the glaciers along the Alaska coast, a seaplane caught up with the ship, and a long message, in code, was handed to the president. The message came from Washington. "After reading it," said Adams, "he suffered something like a collapse." The old indigestion took hold of him again.

He retreated to his stateroom and asked Hoover to join him there. The moment Hoover entered the stateroom, Harding "plumped" a question at him: "If you knew of a great scandal in our administration, would you for the good of the country and the party expose it publicly or would you bury it?"

"Publish it," said Hoover, "and at least get credit for integrity on your side."

Harding said that it might be "politically dangerous."

Harding was the first president to make a radio broadcast, although, as he prepares to do it on the first leg of his Voyage of Understanding, he is evidently not too happy about it.

Hoover asked for more particulars. The president said, as Hoover recalled, "that he had received some rumors of irregularities, centering around Smith, in connection with cases in the Department of Justice. . . . Harding gave me no information about what Smith had been up to. I asked what Daugherty's relations to the affair were. He abruptly dried up. . . ."

Harding told no one what the message contained, nor from whom it had come. The message itself was destroyed, and no one has since been able to trace it. It may have dealt with an indiscretion of Jess Smith's—apparently involving Daugherty: it could have been any one of so many things, something involving fight films or the American Metals case or some oil deal. Probably it was something having to do with bootlegging, but it hardly mattered which of Jess's and Harry's schemes it was: one thread would do as well as any other to begin unraveling Harding's adminstration.

Just at the moment that Harding had decided—however imperfectly, with whatever lack of practice or imagination or energy—to surpass himself, he was seized and held by his past.

Harding began to come apart. As the ship came in through heavy fog to Puget Sound, it struck a destroyer amidships with a terrible crash, and the cry went up for "All hands on deck!" Harding's valet found the president in his stateroom, lying on his bunk, his face buried in his hands. Harding remained motionless and, without looking up, asked his valet what had happened. When told of the accident, he said quietly, his head still buried in his hands, "I hope the boat sinks."

The next day, in Seattle, the president went ashore to deliver a speech to a crowd of 60,000 who had gathered in the city's stadium under a devastating sun. Adams thought the president seemed confused. Others noticed that his face was deeply lined with exhaustion and, it seemed, with pain. When he spoke, referring to his voyage up the coast of Alaska, he hesitated several times, slurred his words, and referred to Alaska as "Nebraska." Halfway through the speech, he faltered, dropped his manuscript, and reached out to grasp the lectern to hold himself erect. Hoover, who had been sitting just

In Alaska, Harding stands atop a rocky promontory and points jauntily nowhere for the sake of a newspaper photographer.

behind the president, reached down, picked up the pages from the floor, and handed them back to the president. It seemed to Adams for a moment as though Harding "were going to give up the struggle," but the president mastered his weakness "by an effort of will," and finished.

That night, said Adams, Harding "suffered what was diagnosed as acute indigestion. Surgeon General Sawyer . . . made the diagnosis. . . . Crab meat was identified as the cause of the upset." Harding had been wandering about restlessly the night before and had found Reddy Baldinger, a journalist who had been one of Harding's old newsboys on the Marion *Star*. Baldinger was sitting alone in the dining room with a mess of crabs he had bought for himself, and Harding had joined him to share the crabs and talk of the old days.

Exhausted, his face deeply lined, his jowls sagging, Harding is undone by the news that was brought to him in the midst of his voyage to Alaska.

The president was told to rest, and another of the members of the party, Doctor Joel Boone, took Hoover aside and told him confidentially that Harding was suffering from heart trouble. The president's speaking dates were canceled, but his journey was continued: the party boarded a train for San Francisco, and by the time he arrived at San Francisco Station, on Sunday morning, July 29, Harding thought he felt better, and he spurned a wheelchair and walked, slowly, to a car. "But his skin," said Adams, "grayish and flabby, his gait, torpid and lifeless, were testimony enough to the fact that only courage was sustaining him. The last pictures, taken as he went to the Palace Hotel, show a face beginning to sag, to lose its firm outlines as the muscular structure weakened. He was an old, drawn man, squinting into the sunlight with a painful, determined smile."

Daugherty flew into San Francisco from the capital–on other business, he said–and then, strangely enough, did not see Harding. Although a room was available for him at the Palace Hotel, Daugherty checked in at the St. Francis.

Harding was put to bed at once and a distinguished heart specialist, who had been notified in advance, took over his care. On Monday, Harding took a bad turn. His temperature rose to 102 and his pulse to 120, and according to another San Francisco physician who had been called in, he was rapidly developing bronchial pneumonia. On Tuesday, he seemed better, and by Wednesday, he had

The engineer stands ready to take Harding's body back through the middle of America to Washington, aboard a special presidential train. (Ohio Historical Society)

so recovered that he was sitting up in bed, taking solid food, and reading the newspapers. His temperature was normal, and his pulse rate had dropped down below 100.

By Thursday, Harding felt well enough that he thought he would be able to head for home on Sunday. By late Thursday afternoon, he was saying that he was "out of the woods," although he did feel "so tired, so tired." Daugherty still neglected to pay a visit, though others did. On Thursday evening, Colonel Starling, who had always followed Harding around the golf course to keep track of his side bets, dropped by, and the president told Starling that he only regretted not having caught any fish in Alaska.

After dinner, the Duchess came in to sit by his bed and to read an article to him that had appeared in the *Saturday Evening Post,* a piece about Harding called "A Calm View of a Calm Man." The article said that Harding was following a good, steady course as president. "That's good," Harding said. "Go on; read some more." The Duchess read the article through to the end and then went across the hall to her own room, leaving Harding with his nurse. The nurse, having gone to get a glass of water to give the president with his medication, returned to the room just in time to see Harding, still stitting up in bed, give a slight twitch and then slump to one side, his head falling down to his shoulder, his mouth open.

Epilogue

When Harding died, the members of the Ohio Gang fell apart like planets bereft of the sun. Calvin Coolidge, who had been chosen as an afterthought to be the vice-presidential candidate at the 1920 Republican convention, succeeded to the office of president, and suddenly probity was the fashion in Washington.

Charlie Forbes became the subject of a congressional investigation almost at once. "I worked sixteen long hours a day," he said in his own defense, naturally counting in the hours of his social drinking, flattering, flirting, and seducing, "and I have been charged," he said with a charming inability to focus on just what the charges were, "with inefficiency; but I will stake my education against anyone who has made that charge of inefficiency against me."

Forbes felt he had not been truly understood. Whatever technicalities of law he might have violated–as had, lamentably, lots of others–he thought, after all, his feelings ought to be taken into account, for, as far as his intentions were concerned, he was absolutely pure: "no man," he said with conviction, "loved the ex-serviceman any better than I did." And yet, nothing saved him. The blackening of his reputation proceeded. He concluded at last that Mortimer and Doc Sawyer had engaged in some sort of conspiracy against him, or–more likely–that he had fallen victim to "politics."

In the winter of 1924–25, he was tried and convicted on the charges of bribery and conspiracy, fined $10,000, and sentenced to two years in Leavenworth.

As for Albert Fall, Harry Sinclair, and Edward Doheny, another congressional committee looked into their dealings in painstaking detail. Fall tried at first to run, moving from his ranch to Chicago to New York, trying to dodge subpoenas, taking to drink, and finally checking into a hospital, "too run-down," according to his doctor, to appear before the committee.

Nonetheless, the investigation ground on until all three men–and Doheny's son, who had delivered a bribe to Fall–were all thoroughly discredited and, in the end, brought up for trial in the District of Columbia. In the first trial of Fall and Doheny, the two men were acquitted, though both were chastened. Doheny had begun to look somewhat pale; his cockiness had begun to ring hollow. Fall walked with a cane by this time, slowly, his feet shuffling. The investigations and hearings and trials had begun to wear him down. In another trial, this one of Harry Sinclair for contempt of the Senate (for having refused to answer some questions), Sinclair was sentenced to three months in jail.

In October of 1927, Fall and Sinclair went on trial for criminal conspiracy. By this time, even Sinclair had begun to break under the pressure, and he hired some private detectives to try to fix the jury. The case was thrown out; Sinclair was tried for jury tampering, and sentenced to six months in the Washington Asylum and jail.

Although Sinclair seemed to survive his ordeal with relative ease, Doheny suffered from the trials. During the course of all the investigations, his son had been shot to death by his secretary, and Doheny's heart had been broken. Every time his son's name was mentioned in the course of the trial, Doheny would begin to weep uncontrollably. The jury, taking pity on him, found him innocent of giving a bribe to Fall. Doheny died several years later, in bed, half-mad.

When Fall was tried in the very same court, he was found guilty of receiving the bribe that Doheny had been found innocent of giving him. By the time Fall was brought to trial, he had to be delivered to the courtroom in a wheelchair, with a doctor and a nurse in attendance. It seemed that he was merely staging a plea for sympathy, until, in the first day of the trial, he collapsed with a hemorrhage. Although the lawyers wanted to postpone the trial, Fall insisted on going ahead so that he might be vindicated.

In the end, he was found guilty and sentenced to the state penitentiary in Sante Fe to which he was taken in an ambulance, because he was suffering from arteriosclerosis, tuberculosis, and pleurisy, among other ailments. He survived his sentence, but his Three River Ranch, for which he had done what he had done, so that he might leave something to his children, was sold at a sheriff's auction to pay his debts. He and his wife were evicted from the ranch, and they moved to a small, down-at-heel house in El Paso, where his wife supported the two of them by working in a lunch-room and canning vegetables at home. She died in 1943, he the next year.

Gaston B. Means, the irrepressible liar, was finally brought up on charges of conspiracy, and although he managed to implicate Daugherty, Mellon, and Harding in the course of his defense, he was sent up for two years. Jail did not improve his character. He surfaced again in 1932, when the infamous kidnapping of the Lindbergh baby seized the attention of so many people. Gaston, remembering his old acquaintances from Harding days, got in touch with Evalyn Walsh McLean and told her that he knew right where the Lindbergh baby was. If she would only come up with

$100,000 ransom and a few thousand expenses, he would use his contacts to save the child. Evalyn gave him the money and never saw it again. She did, however, hate to be swindled. Means went on trial for larceny, was sentenced to fifteen years, and died of a heart attack while serving his term at Leavenworth.

George Remus not only went to jail in the Atlanta penitentiary, but he discovered that he was not even able to purchase a parole or reduction of sentence. The rectitude of Mabel Willebrandt prevailed. Remus asked his wife Imogene, who had stayed loyally with him through all his troubles, to try to arrange something through a young fellow named Franklin Dodge, who worked for Mrs. Willebrandt in the Department of Justice. Even though Remus was in jail, Imogene had the resources of a forty or fifty million dollar business–still active, and with a high cash flow–to draw on for spending money.

Imogene got to know the tall, handsome Dodge, but she seemed unable to arrange anything for Remus. Remus served his full term at Atlanta, and although he began to hear nasty rumors about his wife and Dodge, he knew why Imogene was being friendly to Dodge, and so he was not worried. Two days before he was to be released from the penitentiary, he made a point of issuing a statement to the press, saying that he knew that his wife was faithful to him, that he was grateful to her for her loyalty to him, and that he loved her.

The next day, he was informed that Imogene had filed suit for divorce. The following day, when he was released from the Atlanta jail, he was picked up at once by agents who arrested him again and took him on a train to be arraigned in Dayton for "maintaining a nuisance" at Death Valley Farm. Evidently the fix was in after all, but not in his favor.

In time, Remus began to hear rumors that Imogene had transferred some of their properties to Dodge, that Dodge was helping her run the distillery business, and that Imogene and Dodge had hired a hit man to kill Remus.

While Remus had been serving time in the Dayton jail, Imogene had instituted proceedings to have him deported as an undesirable alien. Although Remus thought of himself as a Chicagoan, he had been born in Germany, and his parents had not come to the United States until he was five years old. Government archives seemed to contain no record of the naturalization papers of Remus's father.

When Remus got out of jail, he decided to put himself back in business by stealing 95,000 gallons of his own whiskey from Imogene. Moving a fleet of trucks into one of his warehouses early one morning, Remus was stopped by federal marshals, who protected what had become Imogene's property. With that, his patience broke.

When at last Remus had to appear in court to settle the divorce terms with Imogene, he got up early in the morning and told his chauffeur to take him around to the Alms Hotel, where Imogene was staying with her twenty-year-old daughter. Imogene came out of the hotel at eight o'clock that morning with her daughter and stepped into a waiting cab. Remus told his driver to follow the cab; when Imogene's daughter saw Remus's limousine, she told the cab driver to move faster. Remus began to make frantic signals to have the cab pull over. Imogene told the cab driver to stop. Her daughter told the driver to go faster. Remus shouted at his driver to cut the cab off. The two cars raced through traffic and into Eden Park, with Remus's driver trying to squeeze the cab off the road. At last, speeding down Eden Park Drive, the limousine pulled ahead of the cab, and cut in front of it. Remus jumped out. Imogene's daughter tried to get out the right side of the cab, but her mother pulled her back and opened the door on the left side. Remus ran around the cab, took Imogene by the wrist, and pulled her out into the roadway, shouting, "I'll fix you! I'll fix you."

"Oh, Daddy," Imogene cried, "you know I love you! You know I love you! Daddy, don't do it! Don't do it!"

He put the pistol to her stomach and shot once, and Imogene fell to the ground with a scream.

Her daughter jumped from the cab and took Remus by the

lapels, shouting, "Do you realize what you're doing?"

Remus looked at the girl abstractedly and said quietly, "She can't get away with that."

While Imogene bled to death on the roadway, Remus walked slowly out of the park and caught a cab to the First District Police Station, where he turned himself in.

At his trial, he defended himself, pleading temporary insanity. He presented the story of his marriage, of his jailings, and of his wife's affair with Franklin Dodge, and of the way his wife and Dodge had taken his business, hired a hit man, and tried to have him deported, and he convinced the jury that he had been overtaken by an uncontrollable rage. He was acquitted by the jury and set free.

He was, however, a broken man. His business was in shambles, and he no longer had the energy to start anew. He drifted for some years, and died at last, without much money, in a small house in Kentucky.

Harry Daugherty tried to hold onto his office as attorney general after Harding's death, but a Senate committee began to investigate him again. The committee asked for documents bearing on such issues as bootlegging, the distribution of fight films, oil deals, failure to prosecute large corporations on monopoly cases; but Daugherty declined to produce any documents. When the heat got to be more than Coolidge could bear, he asked for Daugherty's resignation, and Daugherty, protesting his innocence of all charges, gave up his office–grumbling that the senators who started the investigation were "received in the inner Soviet circles as comrades." Under no circumstances, Daugherty said, would he let these fellows see his files; it was a matter of national security.

He spent his last years in Columbus and Palm Beach, regarding himself as a respected elder statesman of the Republican party, whose reputation was not even tarnished by the fact that his brother Mally was sentenced to ten years in the penitentiary for embezzlement, false entries in his books at the Washington Court House bank, and lying to bank examiners. (Happily, Mally's con-

Nan Britton and her daughter, Elizabeth Ann, had this photograph taken in 1931, when Elizabeth Ann was twelve years old. (Wide World Photos)

viction was overturned in the Ohio Court of Appeals.) Harry lived on to 1941, giving him ample time to write his autobiography, which explained everything.

Nan Britton, short of cash as always, married a ship's captain in January of 1924, and then discovered the captain was neither as rich nor as kind as he had pretended. She had the marriage annulled and then turned to the Harding family for financial help. When the family failed to help her or her daughter with a large settlement, she published her memoirs, *The President's Daughter,* which caused a sensation and brought her temporary wealth. Once that money was gone, she settled down at last in Evanston, Illinois, where she worked in an employment agency and raised her daughter. Elizabeth Ann graduated from Sullivan High School in Evanston and was married in 1938 to a man with whom she had three children and settled down in California.

Carrie Phillips persuaded her husband to leave the house–after he had lost most of his money in the Great Depression–and take up residence in a back room of the Hotel Marion. He died in 1939, and she moved on, from the house on Gospel Hill to one closer to Harding's old home. Over the years, she turned increasingly in on herself. She had few friends, then no friends; she stayed always in her house. She supported herself by raising German shepherd dogs. The most she had to do with the outside world was to fight off the board of health when they raised objections to the conditions and the odor of her backyard kennels. By 1956 she was so poor and so disheveled and unable to care for herself, that she was placed, by court order, in the Willetts Home for the Elderly in Marion, where she died in 1960. Her possessions were auctioned off–except for a box of letters found in a locked closet, the letters to her from Harding.

For several weeks after Harding's death, it was said, smoke could be seen rising from the White House chimney. Mrs. Harding was burning the president's papers. She did indeed burn most of the papers she could find–papers from the president's desk, from the wall safe on the second floor, letters, confidential papers, boxes of files, suitcases full of papers, the contents of a safe deposit box. She had started, at first, to look through the files, sort them out, burn whatever might hurt her husband's reputation, save whatever historical documents might cast him in a good light. But she became exhausted and disgusted with the project as time went on. Overcome by fatigue, she would toss boxes onto flames without looking to see what was in them.

She returned to Marion, then, and had the remaining boxes of papers sent on after her. She took up residence at Doc Sawyer's farm, and there she went on with her work on Harding's papers.

Sometimes she would save a part of a letter, tearing off the top or bottom of the page, burning the rest, and in this way she spent her weeks back home–sorting, ripping, and burning.

During the next months, she and Doc Sawyer commiserated with one another as the congressional investigations and newspaper reporters began to savage the Harding years. By September of 1924, Doc Sawyer had died of a heart attack. By November, after a recurrence of her perennial kidney ailment, Mrs. Harding was dead, too, and the Harding era was ended–although, mischievously, the spirit of the Ohio Gang has never died.

Sources

THIS BOOK IS not a novel—nothing in the book is made up, no event, no character, no word of dialogue, at least not by me. Nor is it a work of scholarly history or biography. The best biography of Harding is Francis Russell's *The Shadow of Blooming Grove;* it is not likely to be surpassed; and excellent scholarly work has been done by Andrew Sinclair, among others. I have relied on their work in composing this book.

This book is meant to be a consideration, or essay, with a little of the old soft shoe. As such, it is based on the sources noted below. The reader, however, must share the historian's task of weighing the evidence and deciding whether a conversation reported by Gaston Means or Nan Britton or Roxy Stinson or Harry Daugherty is solid historical evidence, whether it conveys the right sense of things, or is literally true, or wholly made up. I have included such material because it seemed to me that a fable such as this can be held less strictly accountable for the historical facts, providing it has got its moral right.

On occasion, when such sources entirely leave the realm of the plausible, I've abandoned them without qualm. Gaston Means, for instance, says that Mrs. Harding poisoned the president, which is nonsense, even though it helped Gaston's sales.

Aside from the conversations reported in the book, the other material is drawn from sources that most historians–rightly or wrongly–would consider generally reliable.

References can be found in the selected bibliography that follows these notes.

I, The Handshake

For Jess's appearance and clothes, see Means, page 86, and Adams, pages 42 ff. The appearance of the hotel lobby comes from photographs and drawings in the possession of the New-York Historical Society. The information on Gorini and others in the liquor business comes from the testimony of Gorini in the Investigation of the Attorney General.

II, The Little Green House on K Street

See Starling, 172; Werner, 8, 23, 267, and 273; Adams, 235 ff.; Russell, 520–21. For particulars on the bootlegging arrangements, see Gorini's testimony in the Investigation of the Attorney General. For Mannington, see items on him in the New York *Herald Tribune,* May 8, 1924, and the New York *Evening World,* March 22, 1924.

III, The Safe in the Backyard

Means, 66 ff. and 205 ff. See also Russell, 517.

IV, The House on H Street

Giglio, pages 124 ff. is best on Daugherty. For the visitors to the house, see Werner, 255 ff. For the arrangements at the house, see Russell, 450.

Daugherty himself gives a list of his judicial appointees as an appendix to his *The Inside Story of the Harding Tragedy.*

V, The Poker Party

Adams, 233–35; Russell, 446–48; Sullivan, 17 and 306 ff.

VI, Warren Harding's Baby Pictures

See Russell for this and the succeeding chapters on Harding in Marion, pages 27–48 *passim.* For Harding's early years, see also Sinclair, 13–14, and Sullivan, 89.

VII, The Little Nigger

Russell believes these rumors about Harding to be the key to his character and takes the title *The Shadow of Blooming Grove* from this understanding of Harding's life.

VIII, The Happy Booster

See Jack Warwick's magazine article, "Growing Up with Harding."

IX, A Perfect Marriage

See Russell and Warwick.

X, A Short Course in Political Science

Andrew Sinclair is especially good on Ohio politics, pages 27–78, *passim.*

XI, A Close Call

Russell, 166 ff. Harding's letters to Carrie are sealed by court order and cannot be seen, legally.

XII, The World's Most Exclusive Club

Russell, 114 ff.; Sinclair, 27 ff.

XIII, A Girl On His Arm

See Nan Britton, *passim.*

XIV, The Available Man

See Sinclair, *passim.* Harding's letters come from the Harding Papers; see especially his correspondence with Scobey and Jennings, rolls 263 and 261.

XV, A Blessed, Though Quiet, Event

See Nan Britton.

XVI, The Smoke-Filled Room

Russell, 341 ff.; Daugherty, 29 ff.; Sinclair, 136 ff.

XVII, Carrie Takes Another Vacation

Russell, 402.

XVIII, The Front Porch Campaign

Sinclair, 155 ff.

XIX, The Hardings in the White House

Lowry, 17 ff.; White, 617; Adams, 216 ff.; Evalyn Walsh McLean, 220 ff.; Russell, 447 ff.; Sullivan, 30; Starling, 166 ff.

XX, Pillars Of Society

For Hays, see Sinclair, 191; Adams, 261; Lowry, 83-90; for Mellon, see Sinclair, 200 ff. and 250 ff.; Sullivan, 208; Murray, 179-81; Stokes, 75-82 and 91-95; Lowry, 155-58; for Hughes, see Russell, 271; Sinclair, 183, 190, 206; Murray, 356; Lowry, 168-78; for Hoover, see Russell, 425, 473; Adams, 205, 207, 199; Murray, 194-98; for Fall, see Russell, 264 ff. and

491 ff.; White, 620; for Davis, see Sinclair, 186–87, 203, 254–55, and Murray, 103–104; for Wallace, see Murray, 200; Russell, 434, 470, 534; for Weeks, see Russell, 434, 446, 523; Murray, 101–102; for Denby, see Russell, 434–35, 493; Adams, 203 ff.; Sullivan, 296.

XXI, Bribery

Sullivan, 350; Adams, 323–24.

XXII, Corruption

Werner, 291.

XXIII, Bribery and Corruption

Werner, 282 ff.; Sullivan, 224.

XXIV, Jess Smith Returns to Washington Court House

Adams, 45 ff.; Roxy Stinson testimony, Investigations of the Attorney General.

XXV, The King of the Bootleggers

Coffey, 40 ff.

XXVI, Bribery and Corruption and Sex and Suicide

Sullivan, 238; Adams, 284; Werner, 193 ff.

XXVII, More of the Same with the Jap and Harry Mingle

Werner, 286 ff.

XVIII, The Big Oil Rip-Off and the Even Bigger One That Got Away

Werner, 57 ff.; Russell, 489 ff.; Adams, 348 ff.; Sullivan, 320; Noggle, *passim.*

XXIX, The King of the Bootleggers Returns

Coffey, 77 ff.

XXX, Nan Pays a Visit

Nan Britton, 207 ff.

XXXI, The President Remembers His Schoolboy Aspirations

Russell, 460 ff. and 487; White, 616

XXXII, Things Begin to Come Apart: Gaston Means Investigates Nan Britton

Means, 93 ff.

XXXIII, An Incidental Nuisance: The People Rise Up

Sullivan, 154 ff.

XXXIV, The People Crushed

Sinclair, 256 ff.; Daugherty, 115 ff.

XXXV, An Absent-minded Elimination of Free Speech, Assembly, and So Forth

Murray, 255 ff.; Sinclair, 256 ff.

XXXVI, A Little of the Old Soft Soap

Murray, 166–68; Sullivan, 218; Sinclair, 225–30; Russell, 462.

XXXVII, What Gaston Means Found Out

Means, 105 ff.

XXXVIII, No Escape

Means, 139 ff.

XXXIX, The King of the Bootleggers Cashes in His Chips

Coffey, 129 ff.

XL, Things Get Out Of Hand

Russell, 548 ff.; Adams, 266 ff.; Daugherty, 153–54.

XLI, Things Get More Out of Hand: Mr. and Mrs. Harding

Means, 168 ff.; 242 ff.

XLII, Things Get Completely Out of Hand: Jess Smith

Roxy Stinson's testimony in the Investigation of the Attorney General; Sullivan, 237.

XLII, The President Aspires to Surpass Himself

Sinclair, 272–77; Adams, 367–69.

XLIV, The Past Catches Up

Russell, 574 ff.; Adams, 371 ff.; Sinclair, 285 ff.; Hoover, 49.

Selected Bibliography

In addition to to the following secondary works, two sets of original documents were particularly useful: *Investigation of the Honorable Harry M. Daugherty,* Hearings before the Select Committee on Investigations of the Attorney General, U.S. Senate, 68th Congress, 1st Session, 3 volumes, Government Printing Office, 1924; and The Warren G. Harding Papers, which reside in the Ohio Historical Society in Columbus, and to which references are made in the Notes by the roll number of the 263-roll microfilm edition that the society maintains.

Adams, Samuel H. *Incredible Era.* Boston: Houghton Mifflin Co., 1939.

Alderfer, Harold F. "The Personality and Politics of Warren G. Harding." Ph.D. dissertation, Syracuse University, 1928.

Allsop, Kenneth. *The Bootleggers.* London: Hutchinson & Co., 1961.

Britton, Nan. *The President's Daughter.* New York: Elizabeth Ann Guild, 1927.

Chapple, Joseph Mitchell. *Life and Times of Warren G. Harding.* Boston: Chapple Publishing Co., 1924.

Coffey, Thomas. *The Long Thirst.* New York: W. W. Norton & Co., 1975.

Daugherty, Harry M. *The Inside Story of the Harding Tragedy.* New York: Churchill Co., 1932.

Giglio, James N. *Harry M. Daugherty and the Politics of Expediency.* Kent, Ohio: Kent State University Press, 1978.

Gilbert, Clinton. *The Mirrors of Washington.* New York: G. P. Putnam's Sons, 1921.

Hoover, Herbert. *The Memoirs of Herbert Hoover: The Cabinet and the Presidency, 1920–1933.* New York: Macmillan, 1952.

Hoover, Irwin H. (Ike). *Forty-two Years in the White House.* Boston: Houghton Mifflin Co., 1934.

Kohlsaat, H. H. *From McKinley to Harding: Personal Recollections of Our Presidents.* New York: Charles Scribner's Sons, 1923.

Longworth, Alice Roosevelt. *Crowded Hours.* New York: Charles Scribner's Sons, 1933.

Lowry, Edward G. *Washington Close-ups.* Boston: Houghton Mifflin Co., 1921.

McLean, Evalyn Walsh. *Father Struck It Rich.* Boston: Little, Brown & Co., 1936.

Means, Gaston B. *The Strange Death of President Harding.* New York: Guild Publishing Co., 1930.

Noggle, Burl. *Teapot Dome: Oil and Politics in the 1920s.* Baton Rouge: Louisiana State University Press, 1962.

Reily, E. Mont. *The Years of Confusion.* Unpublished manuscript. Columbus, Ohio. The Ohio Historical Society. Harding Papers, Collection 61, Box 1.

Russell, Francis. *The Shadow of Blooming Grove.* New York: McGraw-Hill Book Co., 1968.

Sinclair, Andrew. *The Available Man.* New York: Macmillan, 1965.

Starling, Edmund W. *Starling of the White House.* New York: Simon & Schuster, 1946.

Stoddard, Henry L. *As I Knew Them.* New York: Harper and Brothers, 1927.

Sullivan, Mark. *Our Times.* Vol. 6. New York: Charles Scribner's Sons, 1935.

Werner, Morris R. *Privileged Characters.* New York: R. M. McBride and Co., 1935.

White, William A. *The Autobiography of William Allen White.* New York: Macmillan, 1946.

Index

INDEX